BRINGING OUT
THE BEST IN YOUR CHILD

"This book provides us with practical suggestions for recognizing each child's uniqueness and worth. As a parent this book gives me great hope. As my mom's kid, it helps me understand her discussions with my confused elementary school teachers because I never fit into the 'traditional classroom,' and as a songwriter, it gives me great ideas for songs! This is a refreshing guide to assist each one of us as we bring out the best in our children."

MARY RICE HOPKINS
INTERNATIONALLY KNOWN FAMILY AND CHILDREN'S
RECORDING ARTIST AND MOTHER OF TWO

"Cynthia Tobias and Carol Funk are two of the best friends any parent could have. The continue to winsomely remind us that each of our children has great worth and potential. In this book, the authors give us the tools to discover the real gold in these treasures we call our children."

JANET PARSHALL
NATIONALLY SYNDICATED RADIO TALK SHOW HOST

Bringing Out the Best in Your Child

80 Ways to Focus on
Every Kid's Strengths

Cynthia Ulrich Tobias
and
Carol Funk

Servant Publications
Ann Arbor, Michigan

© 1997 by Cynthia Ulrich Tobias and Carol Funk

Vine Books is an imprint of Servant Publications especially designed to serve evangelical Christians.

Published by Servant Publications
P.O. Box 8617
Ann Arbor, Michigan 48107

Cover design: Left Coast Design, Inc., Portland, Oregon

97 98 99 00 01 10 9 8 7 6 5 4 3 2

Printed in the United States of America
ISBN 1-56955-016-6

LIBRARY OF CONGRESS CATALOGING-IN-PUBLICATION DATA

Tobias, Cynthia Ulrich
    Bringing out the best in your child : 80 ways to focus on every kid's strengths / Cynthia Ulrich Tobias and Carol Funk.
        p.   cm.
    Includes bibliographical references.
    ISBN 1-56955-016-6
    1. Child-rearing.   2. Parent and child.   3. Individuality in children.   I. Funk, Carol.
II. Title.
MZ769.T574   1997
649'.1—dc21   96-54823
                                                                                CIP

Dedication

To MY ENTIRE FAMILY, who patiently endured the stress of deadlines, and to my good friend and outstanding editor, Gwen Ellis, who understands me and loves me anyway.

Cindy Tobias

To MY HUSBAND, JEFF, for his unfailing love and devotion; and to our two sons, Ryan and Paul, whose strengths I appreciate and try to encourage daily; and to my parents, brother, and twin sister for encouraging me from the very beginning.

Carol Funk

Contents

Foreword

I can still recall how I anticipated my first encounter with Cindy Tobias. I was eager to find out more about her; this young mom with an interesting blend of family, vocational, and educational background. I wondered: *What makes this uniquely gifted person—who was once a policewoman, and is now the mother of twins, and a learning styles advocate—tick?*

I was not disappointed by that first meeting! Cindy Tobias is one of the most delightful, gifted, and entertaining people I have ever met. God has imbued her with wit, wisdom, and a style that immediately connects her with audiences. You can almost see her disarmingly sweet smile as you read her books.

As a writer, Cindy knows how to tickle your funny bone and pierce your heart—all on the same page. My wife, Barbara, and I have benefited greatly from her previous books. Now Cindy has teamed up with her colleague, Carol Funk, to write *Bringing Out the Best in Your Child*. As you'll find out in this book, don't mess with them. They are real. They tell it straight.

It's a good thing this book does not sell "by the pound" because there is a "ton" of practical advice on raising children packed between these two covers. This is a book about children and the reality of parenting them daily. It's so real, that on more than one occasion, I wondered if the authors had been spying on our family.

I *really* like this book! Cindy's and Carol's words lift a beleaguered parent's head and bring fresh perspective about their children. The authors remind us of our children's strengths and potential. This book practically equips parents to live out the words of Robert Lewis

Stevenson, who said, "Make the most of the best and the least of the worst."

In *Bringing Out the Best in Your Child*, the authors hammer home a neglected, but much needed, value—accountability. I really like the way they cleverly equip the reader to apply workable solutions every day. In fact, I'm so convinced of the value of this book, that I'm tempted (well, almost tempted) to say that if you, as a parent, don't benefit from its pages, I'll buy it back from you!

I sure hope you will enjoy this book and its authors as much as Barbara and I have.

Dennis Rainey
Executive Director of Family Life
(A division of Campus Crusade for Christ)

A Word from
Cynthia Tobias

Have you ever worried that your children may argue too much or play too rough or rebel against authority? Have you been told that your kids are too restless, too talkative, too inattentive?

Every parent wants the best for each of their children. But how do you know what the best *is*? Why is each child so different? In my first book, *The Way They Learn*, I introduced the term *learning styles*: natural, inborn strengths and characteristics in each individual. Our learning style affects how we perceive, understand, and organize information. It helps us decide what makes sense and what's important. Although the research has been around for decades, the practical application of the concept has recently begun to be widely known and accepted, especially among educators and parents. As parents begin to do their homework, we begin to realize just how unique and wonderful each of our children really is!

My husband, John, and I have "identical" twin boys. Although we realized each boy was different even before they were born, they continue to teach us lessons every day about recognizing and valuing their individuality. I remember one incident in particular, the year before Robert and Michael started kindergarten.

John had picked the boys up at preschool earlier that day. Later in the evening, after we had tucked both boys in, he casually mentioned that the teacher had informed him we needed to counsel both Robert and Michael about standing for the Pledge of Allegiance. "She said the boys refused to stand today, and the more she *in*sisted the more they *re*sisted."

I was surprised. Both boys love reciting the Pledge of Allegiance, and neither boy had ever given their teachers any real trouble as far as I knew. I decided I would take advantage of our early morning snuggling time to discuss the issue.

Mike came in first, about 6:00 A.M. As he burrowed his way under the warm covers, I brought the subject to his attention, all the time remembering the analytic bent of his mind. "Mike, did you have a problem in school yesterday?" He shrugged. "Mike, do you know *why* it's important to stand when we say the Pledge of Allegiance?" He shook his head. "No, why?" I quickly reviewed why we salute the flag and what it stands for, and he nodded his head in understanding. "Mike, do you know why it's so important that we do what our teachers tell us to do?" He shrugged again. "No, why?" I briefly outlined the importance of respecting authority and your elders, and then said, "Mike, it's really important that you stand for the Pledge of Allegiance, OK?" He nodded and replied, "OK." End of discussion.

Robert—my random, big-picture, relational kid—bounced into bed an hour later, snuggling close to me. I was ready to launch into my Pledge of Allegiance lesson. "Robert," I began, "did you have a problem in school yesterday?" He shook his head. "I don't want to talk about it, Mommy." I drew him closer. "Robert, do you know why we stand when..." "Mommy, I didn't *want* to stand." I decided to take another approach. "Robert, do you know why it's important to do what our teachers..." His next words came tumbling out. "Mommy, my teachers don't know me; they don't *know* me!" The intensity of his emotion surprised me. "Robert, what do you mean?" He sat up and looked me in the eye. "One teacher spells my name R-O-B, and I want to be R-O-B-E-R-T." We sat and talked for a few minutes, and I suggested that he tell his teachers how he felt, and ask to have them spell his name the way he preferred. He agreed to talk to his teachers, and the issue of standing at the appropriate time became completely irrelevant.

Although both boys like school, Mike doesn't count on having the teachers like him. If they do, he's thrilled, but if they don't, he just figures it's *their* problem and he goes on about his business. Robert, on the other hand, is absolutely dependent upon personal daily contact with his teacher. Each day he comes in, he first stops her and tugs on her arm. "Mrs. Rosson, I need to tell you something!" Mrs. Rosson stoops down and listens to what is usually a very minor detail about his day, gets a quick hug, and sends him on to his table. Robert feels connected, and happily begins his tasks.

How can two boys, born two minutes apart, who look so much alike, be so different? I never cease to be amazed at my own in-home "laboratory." Every day I marvel that these boys so consistently demonstrate to me the need to communicate information in a variety of ways. I am so blessed to have these small and wonderful reminders of the complexity and uniqueness God gave each of us. I hope I never get used to the differences; I want always to remember to appreciate and value each of my children for who he is, and the strengths he possesses.

The following chapters are designed to give you some practical ideas for recognizing and appreciating the individuality of each of your children. Even children growing up in the very same family at the very same time can be dramatically different in the way they learn and understand and communicate. Although it may seem like your child is *deliberately* trying to annoy you, it helps to remember that he or she probably has a very different perspective on the world.

I have to admit, it's often exhausting to identify and work with the unique strengths and characteristics of each child. But, speaking from personal experience, I believe you will *love* the results!

A Word from
Carol Funk

When I think back to my own childhood, my parents had to deal with twins, just as Cindy and John do. But their experience was very different from that of the Tobias family. Mike and Robert Tobias are pre-wired very differently. My twin sister Cathy and I were two peas in a pod. Our appearance gave no clue to our identity, and neither did our behavior. When we were babies, Mom had a piece of yarn tied around an ankle of one of us so she could tell us apart. Then one day it floated off in the bathtub! Now which twin was which? Even the police couldn't make a positive identification based on footprints. So Mom reassigned our names and started over!

Our learning styles were exactly the same. Not only did we look alike down to our toes, but we acted and reacted alike. We wore identical clothes. Our voices sounded similar. We got sick at the same time. And yet, we wanted to be treated as individuals. We resented teachers who called us by the wrong name because they couldn't tell us apart. Cathy and Carol. We loved being twins, but we still wanted to be appreciated for our individuality. I began to understand why when I met Cindy and first heard about learning styles.

I was awestruck when I first heard the learning style message several years ago. My first response was, *I wish I had known about learning styles when my children were toddlers!* It also gave me insight into the twin issue I had faced my whole life. I needed to be understood as an individual. My second response was a little more sobering. *How could it be that I, a well-educated, successful instructor, preparing college undergraduates to enter the teaching profession, had never heard any of this learning styles material?* Needless to say, I wrote a new job description!

As I began applying learning styles to our family, I suddenly realized that my husband and two boys were wired with strengths very different from mine. I began to appreciate, in a new way, the uniqueness of our family of four. Small, but natural, conflicts between us began to diminish as I refocused my role in light of learning styles. As a wife, I realized that Jeff's style brought balance to mine. We are truly blessed to have each other and to be a team. As a mother, I became more accepting and tolerant of the boys' preschool behavior as I watched for strengths, rather than focusing on weaknesses. I observed the way they played, the toys they liked, the books they wanted to have read to them. All were small indicators of their individual preferences. As Ryan and Paul entered school, I sought teachers who would value and develop their natural strengths.

Perhaps the most amazing transformation occurred in my classroom. I suddenly realized that my "learning style" was also my "teaching style." If I truly wanted to teach so that students were learning well, I had to expand my lessons to account for all the learning styles in the classroom. I needed to stretch my methods and communicate in a variety of styles so a greater portion of my students would understand and learn. I awoke to the reality that I wanted "learners" in class, not just "students." Many of the students who experienced the revolution in my teaching style that academic year, would later testify to the impact it made in their careers. They saw me put into practice what I believed, that understanding learning styles is the key to better teaching. The ultimate compliment came from a student the following year. "Mrs. Funk," Louise said, "I think of my other teachers and my other classes in black-and-white, but I think of this class and you in color!"

Louise's testimony is one of many that demonstrates the profound effect that coming to understand learning styles has had in my life. I began the journey of recognizing and appreciating the strengths of every person in my family and then took it off-site to my classroom. I'm not a perfect parent or a nationally recognized teacher, but it does make a positive impact every time I practice what I teach.

I join with Cindy to encourage you as you recognize and build on the strengths of your child. Regardless of how similar or how different your child or children may be, try to remember that each of us is uniquely created, uniquely gifted, and uniquely special.

A Word from Both of Us

If your child does not fit into a traditional classroom, it is not necessarily an indication that he or she has a learning disability. If your child is strong willed, it does not necessarily mean that he or she is being rebellious or defiant. Sometimes the traits and behaviors that seem most frustrating and annoying in your child can actually be indicators of positive strengths and future success.

As you read this book, you will undoubtedly recognize many of the situations we describe. In virtually every circumstance, what appears to be a drawback in a child's behavior can actually be seen as a strength from the perspective of their learning style. But how can you tell the difference between honoring their individuality and simply letting them get by with too much? Before you begin to read the book, we'd like to give you a few basic tenets of our philosophy regarding discipline and bottom line accountability.

Recognizing and appreciating individual strengths and learning styles does not excuse misbehavior or give license to do whatever an individual feels like doing. There are standards of conduct and rules of behavior that must stay in place, regardless of what may or may not be comfortable for a child. Certain rules stay non-negotiable, such as those that deal with physical safety and moral values. Wrong is wrong, regardless of learning style preferences. But the effectiveness of how you communicate and enforce those rules will be significantly improved when you honor your child's learning style strengths.

Virtually all children respond better to positive rewards, praise, and encouragement than they do to threats, guilt, or coercion. When parents really know and understand each individual child, they can design strategies and instruction using rewards that truly motivate that child to succeed.

Not every situation or circumstance you encounter as a parent can be defined by learning style traits. There are times when a problem goes *beyond* style. It may indicate a medical, neurological, or psychological cause. When these other factors come into play, we encourage you to seek professional help, realizing your child still has learning strengths to be appreciated and used as a strong foundation.

We hope that by the time you finish reading these stories, you will have a better understanding of practical ways to help your child succeed by working *with* his or her learning strengths rather than working against them. If you can do this, *both* you and your child will be happier, and your child will gain the skills and confidence to live a rich and fulfilling life!

∼ 1 ∼

I Get the Front Seat!

"Dibs on the front seat!" Kyle raced out the door toward the car.

"No way!" roared his older sister, Shari. "You got it last time—it's my turn!"

"Hey! What about me?" their youngest brother Earl cried. "I never get the front seat!"

"ENOUGH!" shouted their mother. "No one gets it!"

"That's not fair!" they chorused. As they began wrestling with each other, Jean Gibson had to practically scream to get their attention.

"I mean it! All three of you get in that back seat now!"

They scrambled into the back seat.

"I get the window!"

"No sir! You got the window last time—I get the window!"

"But I never get the window! Move over!"

"Mom! Make him give me the window seat!"

Jean closed her eyes for a moment and prayed for more patience. Then she calmly got out of the car.

"Hey, Mom, where are you going?" All three children looked surprised. Jean walked into the house without comment, and returned a few moments later. The kids had stopped arguing, wondering what their mother had in mind.

Jean opened the back door of the car and addressed her children pleasantly.

"OK. From now on, we have a new method for deciding who gets what seat." She showed them what she had brought from the house. It was the cardboard spinner from one of their board games. She took a pen from her purse, and labeled each color on the spinner as one of the seat positions in the car. The extra spaces were labeled "spin again."

The children looked puzzled. Jean held out the spinner. "All three of you have more energy and enthusiasm than I do. So here's what we're going to do to help you channel your powers of persuasion and negotiation into a calmer method. Earl, you're the youngest, so today you get to spin first. Next time Kyle will spin first, then Shari will go first. We'll keep rotating by age. Whatever seat you spin, you get—no trading or arguing."

Earl gave the wheel an enthusiastic spin. "Middle seat! Oh, man!" His mother took the spinner and handed it to his brother.

"There's always next time, Earl." As each child spun for their seat, Jean felt pleased. *Peace at last!* she thought.

As they drove away, Kyle leaned toward the front seat.

"Hey, Mom, do you think we could do this spinner thing for who sits where at dinner? Hey, how about we spin to decide what we have for dinner?"

Jean smiled and shook her head. "Don't push your luck, Kyle."

"Yeah, that's a stupid idea, Kyle!" Shari said.

"It is not!" Kyle replied.

"Is too!"

"Is not!"

Jean sighed. Maybe she could talk her husband into spinning the wheel to see who drove the kids to school.

Recognize the Strength

Even though it is annoying, energetic kids who actively interact with their siblings are exhibiting very normal behavior. Taking advantage of their energy and enthusiasm will be easier than demanding they simply quiet down and do it your way. Staying calm and doing something they don't expect almost always gets their attention. High energy and lots of enthusiasm are a real plus in life.

Focus on Accountability

In this instance, it's very important that Mom stay in charge. Although some arguing is normal for brothers and sisters, it can quickly become counterproductive if the noise level and physical wrestling escalate. Let the kids know who's in charge, but give them some options that allow each of them to share a little of the control. In this story the spinner gives everyone an equal chance of getting the front seat, but Mom controls the spinner.

∼ 2 ∼

Have You Done Your Homework?

The note from Tracy's teacher was totally unexpected. Her dad called her into the living room and held out the piece of white paper.

"Tracy, your teacher says you haven't done your homework all week. You told me every night that you *had* done all your assignments. Did you lie to me?"

The surprised third grader shook her head vigorously and tears sprang to her eyes. "No, Daddy. I *did* my homework—honest!"

Her father looked puzzled. "Why, then, would your teacher tell me the homework is missing? Did you turn it in?"

Tracy looked uncomfortable. "Well, I turned in the homework I *did*," she said, "but it might not have been exactly what the teacher wanted."

Tracy's dad put his arm around her. "Why don't we compare this list of assignments to the papers you finished?" he suggested. Tracy reluctantly pulled the papers out of her notebook, and together, father and daughter began to compare them to the list the teacher had sent home.

"Tracy, Monday's social studies assignment was supposed to be about the natural resources in Savannah, Georgia. But the homework you turned in is all about raising corn in the Midwest. Did you misunderstand?"

Tracy shrugged. "No," she admitted, "but I thought *my* subject was more interesting. I wanted to know more about my favorite vegetable—corn on the cob."

Her dad smiled in spite of himself. "Tracy, do you know why you need to *do* your assigned homework?"

Tracy brightened. "Oh, yes! It helps you learn more about what you want to know!"

24

"Actually, Tracy," her dad explained patiently, "it helps you understand what your *teacher* wants you to know."

Tracy frowned. "But that's too *boring!*" she protested.

"Well," her dad countered, "why don't we figure out how we could make your teacher's homework seem *less* boring." He and Tracy took another look at the teacher's list of assignments. They began to make a game of trying to figure out what might be the most interesting part of each assignment. Over the next few weeks, both of them learned to ask the right questions. Tracy asked her teacher to help her figure out what could make the homework interesting, and her dad learned to ask Tracy if she had done the *assigned* homework!

Recognize the Strength

Creativity combined with practicality helped Tracy get her homework done, even though what she did wasn't technically what her teacher had assigned. As they learned to work together, Tracy's resourcefulness also helped her teacher view her completed homework from a whole new perspective!

Focus on Accountability

Homework and the battles it often causes can be a major source of stress in a home. The goal is to help the child accomplish the assigned task that has been designed to reinforce classroom learning. The key to success lies in matching the task to the learner. Tracy and her father were able to pick out an interesting aspect of each homework assignment so that Tracy could complete the tasks and also have a vested interest in meeting the goal. Working with the teacher in this instance also helped clear the lines of communication and prevented misunderstandings among everyone involved.

～ 3 ～

Too Rough on the Playground

"Richard grabbed a kid on the playground and began choking him. They were playing way too rough. His behavior is beginning to show a very aggressive pattern."

Mrs. Tyler was listening with a mixture of surprise and concern to Richard's teacher explain why he had received a formal warning. Richard loved kindergarten, mostly because he really liked being with his new friends. He was large for his age and sometimes got carried away when he was playing with the other children. He had a very tender heart, and his mother knew what a loving personality he possessed. She sighed and apologized to the teacher. "I'll talk to Richard," she promised, wondering how she could make her five year old understand that his strength and enthusiasm could make him both loved and feared among his classmates.

Over dinner that evening, Mrs. Tyler introduced the subject of Richard's warning at school that day. Richard's eyes filled with tears. "Mommy, I'm sorry. I'll be good next time, I promise!"

Mrs. Tyler smiled. "I know you always try, sweetheart. Sometimes you just forget that you can hurt someone without even meaning to do it. You need to be very careful not to hit or be rough with your friends."

Richard frowned. "But, Mommy, Christopher took the toy I wanted and he wouldn't give it to me. He's supposed to *share!*"

Mrs. Tyler put her arm around him. "Richard, was grabbing Christopher worth being punished and feeling bad?" Richard shook his head vigorously. He didn't think so. "Then you need to say to yourself: 'It's not worth it,' and walk away when you feel angry and want to hurt someone."

Richard's face brightened. "It's not worth it!" he said happily. His mom nodded. "Richard, let's practice. Pretend I'm another kid and I grab your ball. How do you feel?"

"I'm mad." Richard stuck out his bottom lip.

"But what are you going to say?"

"It's not worth it!" he replied.

"That's right," Mrs. Tyler said. "And in the future, if you feel yourself getting really mad and you know you'll get in trouble if you do what you feel like doing, what will you say?"

"It's not worth it!"

The next morning before school, Mrs. Tyler wondered if Richard would remember his newfound resolve. Just before he entered his classroom, she whispered in his ear: "What do you say if something's going to happen that might get you in trouble?" He grinned from ear to ear and threw his arms around her neck.

"It's not worth it!" he said as he planted a big wet kiss on her cheek.

Recognize the Strength

A sweet spirit and tender heart will gain great favor and last longer as a child learns how to harness emotions and negotiate peacefully. A child who is greatly concerned with how he is perceived by others will naturally develop a "sixth sense" when it comes to eliciting cooperation from others.

Focus on Accountability

Helping a child make choices regarding appropriate conduct is one of the most demanding parts of child rearing. As we constantly work toward grooming their behavior, it is important to help children understand, in their own terms, the "what" and "why" of how we treat others. They need to know how our behavior and attitudes affect the people around us. Role playing, such as Richard's mother used, often helps children practice how to act or talk, and gives them immediate feedback when putting new methods to work. It will be important to consistently review and role play this option with the child. Children need to practice with you to gain skills for getting along with others. Changing aggressive behavior is generally not a quick fix, and the child may have difficulty putting skills into practice with success every time. Modeling patience and persistence will go a long way toward cultivating a positive relationship between you and your child.

～4～

Don't Use That Language!

"Shut up!" Rachel was screaming at the top of her voice, and her younger brother was quickly ducking out of her room to escape her wrath. Rachel's mom listened to the exchange of words in despair. It seemed as if she had tried everything to get her eleven-year-old daughter to treat her brother and other family members with courtesy and respect. Particularly distressing was Rachel's habitual use of that annoying phrase *Shut up*. Rachel's parents had already used a variety of disciplinary techniques—without success—to erase those words from her vocabulary. Today's transgression was the last straw.

"Rachel! You come down here *this instant!*" Rachel could tell her mother meant business, but she still took her time getting to the kitchen for the confrontation. When she walked in, she saw her mother standing beside the kitchen table, holding a large piggy bank. *Uh oh,* she thought, *this might have something to do with my allowance.*

Mom knew that Rachel loved shopping, and the money she received each week for doing chores around the house was very important to Rachel and her bank account. This was Mom's last hope for getting her headstrong, impulsive daughter to stop and think about saying that disturbingly rude phrase. As Rachel entered the kitchen, Mom took a deep breath and began.

"Rachel, your father and I have told you over and over not to use the phrase *Shut up*. You have promised us several times that you would not say it again, but you keep breaking your promise. I didn't want to have to do this, but from now on we will be charging you money every time you use it. Each time you say *Shut up*, you'll need to put a dime in this piggy bank. Perhaps now you'll stop and think before you decide to keep using such rude language."

Rachel looked at her mom without saying anything, then abruptly turned and went up to her room. Her mom was puzzled. This wasn't like Rachel. Usually she argued and protested and complained about the lack of fairness in her punishments. Did she understand this latest judgment? Did she realize what violating this agreement could potentially cost her?

It was only a matter of minutes before Rachel reappeared in the kitchen. She was holding two big handfuls of coins, obviously taken from her piggy bank upstairs. Unceremoniously, she dumped all the coins on the kitchen table next to her mother.

"There!" she stated. "Here's all the money I have. Now I can say *Shut up* as many times as I want to."

Rachel's mom was momentarily stunned. This was *not* the way this whole thing was supposed to turn out! Thanks to her own proposal, her daughter had just purchased the right to say the forbidden phrase without being punished for it. Fighting the urge to lose her temper, Rachel's mom remained calm and smiled at her defiant offspring.

"Well, Rachel, you got me. I have to admit, you're two steps ahead of me a lot of the time. This is certainly proof that you have an extremely resourceful and creative mind. Let's start over."

Rachel seemed to be caught off guard with her mother's quiet admission. She reluctantly sat down where her mother indicated and actually seemed to be listening as she spoke.

"Rachel, you are one of the most persuasive people I know. Your friends and family love and admire you. But I don't think you realize that saying *Shut up* to people hurts them and makes them feel less valued by you. I also think you truly want to make an effort to quit saying it so much. So you tell me. What do you think it will take to get you to stop using that phrase?"

Rachel was surprised. She had been prepared to argue, to defend her right to free speech, and to "die" for her cause. But she hadn't expected *this*. For a few moments, she was actually speechless. When she did speak, she seemed thoughtful. "Well, I want you to quit bugging me so much about saying it," she replied. "I don't think it's all that bad. I mean, I could say a lot *worse* things." Her mom struggled to keep silent. Rachel continued. "I don't think it's fair to charge me money for saying it. But I guess we could think of something that would remind me not to use it so much when I talk."

Her mom nodded. "Like what?"

Rachel thought for a moment. "How about when I accidentally forget and say *Shut up,* you could just say *Open down,* and I would know what you mean? Then you could just drop it." Rachel's mom smiled and fought the urge to say any more than three words: "It's a deal."

Rachel's mom knew there was a good chance that she and her daughter would be renegotiating a few days from now. But, for those few days, she *and* Rachel would be learning a little more about compromise and accountability.

Recognize the Strength

Quick thinking and a sharp wit such as Rachel's is a real asset in the adult world, especially in problem-solving and decision-making. Resourcefulness and resilience will keep our children flexible and adaptable to changing circumstances.

Focus on Accountability

One of the best ways to solve a problem is to have direct input from those involved. In this case, Rachel's mother admitted to needing a "start-over" and asked Rachel to help create a solution to the problem. Often, when a strong-willed, determined child is given an ultimatum, the child knows you cannot *force* compliance, and simply calls your bluff. It often helps to "lighten up" and choose your battles. Keep the lines of communication open by seeking appropriate alternatives and respecting the quick thinker. If you are careful to define the goals, you may be amazed at the creative ways the outcomes will be met!

~ 5 ~

Do I Have To Tell You Everything?

"Mrs. Russell, are we supposed to learn all these spelling words? Did you say we should write them five times? Can I use my purple pen instead of my blue one? Does it matter if we print or if we write cursive?"

Althea Russell fought the urge to show how exasperated she really felt. How could one fourth grader demand so much attention *every* day? How many times would she have to give Stephen Curtis the directions before he would just get *busy* and do his work? Stephen was waiting.

"Oh, Stephen, for heaven's sake, stop worrying about so many details. *Yes*, learn all the spelling words. *Yes*, write them five times. I don't *care* what ink you use, and I don't *care* if you write or print. Now *get started!*" Stephen looked hurt, but he walked back to his desk and started his assignment. Mrs. Russell was glad her parent-teacher conference with Stephen's father was this afternoon. She needed to encourage his dad to help Stephen feel more secure about doing his schoolwork independently.

A few hours later, Mr. Curtis listened as Mrs. Russell recounted Stephen's frequent requests for clarification on virtually every assignment or task. Mr. Curtis smiled.

"Isn't it great that Stephen has such an eye for detail? You know, his mother and I think he may make a great surgeon someday—or maybe an accountant or an engineer. We feel pretty sure he's going to make a significant contribution to the world."

Mrs. Russell felt frustrated. Didn't his father understand how annoying it was being asked a thousand times to repeat something he should have gotten the first time? She tried to ask the question politely.

"Mr. Curtis, have you noticed how difficult it seems to be for Stephen to do his work until he's asked for an explanation about almost every detail of the assignment?"

Stephen's dad nodded. "Actually, he asks his mom a lot more questions than he asks me. I guess it's because she assumes he understands a lot more than he actually does. She figures if she just gives him the main idea or a place to start, he'll go ahead and fill in the question marks on his own. I probably give him too *much* information, because I tend to leave *nothing* to his imagination."

Mrs. Russell felt a small pang of guilt. She *did* assume a lot on the part of her students. After all, she *wanted* them to learn to think for themselves.

"I don't always give my students every detail," she admitted. "I guess I'm often not as specific as Stephen needs me to be when it comes to giving directions."

Mr. Curtis grinned. "Mrs. Russell, you're one of the best teachers Stephen's had so far. He's really learned a lot from you. He *does* struggle sometimes to make sure he's doing exactly what you want him to do, but it's just because your approval is so important to him."

At the conclusion of the conference, Mrs. Russell stood to shake Mr. Curtis' hand. "Mr. Curtis, I think maybe I'm learning as much from Stephen as he's learning from me." Stephen's dad nodded. "He's teaching me a few things, too," he admitted.

Recognize the Strength

Stephen's clear thinking, predictability, and natural bent to focus on specific detail will be a real asset to him, especially in the future. His tendency to clarify and define what he learns will help him understand and assimilate new information quickly.

Focus on Accountability

Some children have a need for clear and specific instructions. Parents and teachers can help by giving as much detail as possible from the very beginning of the instructions. When children ask for clarification, help them recognize that there are times when they will need to figure out some of the details for themselves. Role play two or three situations and encourage the child to try the new skill he or she is learning. Try giving children a set of rather general instructions, and then let them try their hand at filling in the details. Then compare what they came up with to what you actually had in mind.

～ 6 ～

Are You Daydreaming Again?

"Carolyn, will you answer the question, please?" Mrs. Ryan, the ninth-grade history teacher, was standing by Carolyn's desk, and the whole class had turned in her direction.

Carolyn blushed and felt tears coming to her eyes. Was Mrs. Ryan going to embarrass her in front of her classmates? Then she felt angry with herself. *You should have been listening,* she scolded herself silently. *Now you're in trouble.*

Mrs. Ryan was speaking again. "Carolyn, I can tell you weren't paying attention. What were you thinking?"

Carolyn paused to consider the situation. Maybe she should try telling Mrs. Ryan the truth this time. The other kids would laugh at her anyway.

"Well," Carolyn said, "you were talking about the early settlers and the Church and how hundreds of missionaries had been sent out to work in the cornfields. I guess I was just wondering who *lived* in the cornfields, and why we would send people there in the first place."

Mrs. Ryan looked puzzled for a moment, wondering why in the world Carolyn was talking about *cornfields.* Then she struggled to keep from laughing. Her mind raced, wondering how she could spare Carolyn from the ridicule of her classmates.

"Carolyn," she began, "I absolutely *love* your sense of humor! You have a wonderful sense of imagination. Not many in this class would have even thought about the connection between the missionaries going to *foreign* fields and *corn* fields!"

As the whole class laughed, Mrs. Ryan moved quickly on to the next point and left Carolyn to concentrate on how to pay attention to the rest of the lecture. After class, Mrs. Ryan asked Carolyn to stay behind for just a moment.

"Carolyn, I meant it when I said you have a wonderful imagination. But I think sometimes it interferes with your ability to listen and remember what we talk about in class."

Carolyn looked down at her feet, and tried not to show how guilty she felt. Mrs. Ryan continued.

"Carolyn, it made a big difference today when you decided to tell me what you were actually thinking. Once I understood why your mind wandered in the first place, I could clear up the misunderstanding so you could concentrate. It would be helpful to me if you would do that more often. I don't always think about the pictures my words conjure up in the mind of someone who is as literal as you are. I think the whole class would benefit by having you point out the possibilities so we can all focus on an accurate image."

Carolyn looked doubtful. "I don't want the other kids to laugh at me," she protested.

Mrs. Ryan shook her head. "I don't believe they will," she said. "I think they'll actually enjoy it, and even join in. We may even be able to make history come alive by occasionally having a sense of humor."

Carolyn shrugged. "I just thought I was pretty stupid."

Mrs. Ryan reached out and squeezed her arm reassuringly. "Oh, Carolyn, think how many other kids probably feel that way, too! Let's see if we can't help everyone feel better about history *and* themselves!"

As Carolyn left the classroom, she shook her head in disbelief. Who would have thought she'd end up using something that usually got her in trouble to actually improve her standing in history class?

Recognize the Strength

The ability to create a vivid mental image while learning new information can help greatly in the recall of that data later. Whether your child needs to memorize facts for a formal test or simply keep an idea alive, if he or she tends to have a highly visual imagination, you can capitalize on the power of the mental image.

Focus on Accountability

When children like Carolyn create a mental picture in this way, it can often look like inattention or daydreaming. These children are actively listening, while their mind is "drawing." Fostering this spatial imagination by encouraging the child to doodle or illustrate in the margins of class notes may help them stay more closely tuned to the teacher, while giving them the freedom to visualize information they need to remember.

～ 7 ～

You Talk Too Much

"Dad, did I leave my books in here?" Thirteen-year-old Debra entered the room breathlessly. Without giving her dad a chance to respond, she continued. "I know I had them before I went to my piano lesson, but I think I put them on the kitchen table. Oh, wait, maybe Mom put them in my bedroom—no, she'd never find an empty place to set them down in there! I wonder if Angela took them by mistake or if Robert stopped to borrow them so he could catch up on his homework. He was absent yesterday, you know, and I promised to help him with his makeup work. Oh, Dad, do you think I could go to the library tonight and help him with his assignment? Oh, never mind, I forgot we have soccer practice. Hey, I know: could he just come over for dinner? Is Mom home yet?"

"*Debra!*" Her dad raised his arms in a "time out" gesture. "Enough! I give up! Stop talking!"

Debra looked surprised at his frustration.

"Debra, how many questions did you just ask me?"

She looked puzzled, and then replied. "One. Is Mom home yet?"

He shook his head in amazement.

"You must have asked at least half a dozen questions just now," he told her. "Is that last one the *only* one you really wanted *answered?*"

She nodded, still surprised by his response.

"Debra, why do you think you talk so much?"

She shrugged.

"Dad, I just need to *think,* that's all. I guess maybe I'm just thinking out loud."

Her dad smiled and put his arm around her.

"Deb, I've got an idea. What if we come up with a code word? When you're just thinking out loud, I won't even try to listen or make sense of what you're saying until you mention the code word. Then I'll listen very carefully to everything you say after that."

"Dad, you're so weird!" she protested. "I can't think of a word!"

"Oh, Debra, you think of *thousands* of words! Just pick one that will always mean that what you say next will be really important."

She sighed, and thought for a moment. "OK, how about I just say *weird* and from then on you'll really listen to me. Dad? Dad? Are you listening? Hey! *Weird!* Will that work?"

Her dad grinned and hugged her. "Well, it might take some practice, but I'll bet it will help us get along better. After all, I won't bug you about talking too much, and you'll know I'm listening when it's important to you that I answer."

"Whatever!" she said.

"Was I supposed to listen to that?" her dad teased. "I didn't hear the code!"

"Oh Dad, you're so *weird!*"

Recognize the Strength

The ability to express her thoughts and feelings will be a distinct advantage to Debra as she matures. As she talks through problems, she'll be able to clarify what she's thinking, and identify what's important to her. Debra may become a real asset in brainstorming sessions where ideas are put forth at random and then sorted through to see what works.

Focus on Accountability

Some very verbal children may need to know how they sound to those around them who aren't so vocal. Perhaps using a tape recorder so the verbal child can listen to his or her own voice and rambling conversations can help put that verbal nature in perspective. A code word is a good idea, and the child may even be encouraged to share it with teachers or friends at school.

~ 8 ~

Stop Arguing with Me

It was the Snyders' weekly family conference, and things weren't going too well. Amy, their seventeen-year-old daughter, seemed especially argumentative tonight, and her eleven-year-old brother, Jason, was becoming defensive and withdrawn.

"You argue about *everything!*" Jason shouted, looking at Amy accusingly.

"I do *not!*" she replied angrily. "I just need to understand what you guys are *talking* about!"

Mrs. Snyder had been listening with a growing sense of despair and frustration. Suddenly she sat up straight in her chair and looked her daughter directly in the eye.

"Wait a minute," she said quietly. "Amy, *why* did you say you argued with Jason?"

"I *told* you!" Amy cried. "I'm just trying to figure out what's going *on!*"

Her mom nodded her head. "Amy, I wonder if you actually *argue* in order to *learn?*"

Amy frowned. "What do you mean?"

"Well," her mother replied, "it seems that every time we try to communicate information to you, we end up in an argument. I don't believe it's because you dislike us that much, so I'm just wondering if you argue because that's how you try to make sense of the information."

Amy paused. "I don't dislike you," she said. Then she looked at her brother and grinned. "Well, *sometimes* I do. But even my friends say I argue too much. I don't think I do. Maybe the questions I ask just make me sound like I'm criticizing or being mean."

Mrs. Snyder put her arm around her daughter and addressed the rest of the family. "Hey, guys, how about we agree to try and communicate what we want as clearly as possible, and then try not to take Amy's questions quite so personally?" Jason and his dad both nodded, and Amy looked relieved.

"What if it doesn't work?" Amy asked. "What happens then?"

Jason jumped to his feet. "See? You're already asking negative questions!" Then he smiled. "Just testing, Amy!"

Recognize the Strength

While it often sounds as if she's just trying to pick a fight, Amy has an honesty in her verbal communication that can be viewed as frank and open. Her keen desire to learn keeps her questioning those around her. She wants to know more about almost everything.

Focus on Accountability

Just as Amy's frank and open questioning can be viewed as honesty, it can also be mistaken for disrespect and hostility. Try to guide children like Amy to speech class or a debate team where the guidance of a good coach can help refine and direct the verbal dueling skills to diplomatic and socially acceptable outcomes. This could be the making of a great student body officer or the beginning of a political career.

～ 9 ～

Is it Normal to Be So Quiet?

"Where's Dennis?" Mr. Conner was adding the final touch to the spaghetti sauce while his wife set the table. Mrs. Conner sighed.

"He's in his room working on his computer again. Honestly, it's a good thing he gets hungry occasionally or we'd *never* see him."

Mr. Conner frowned. "Do you think it's normal for a ten-year-old boy to be alone so much? Shouldn't he be spending more time with his friends?"

"Actually," his wife said, "I asked Dennis' teacher about that yesterday. She said he's pretty quiet in class, too. But she told me that Dennis seems to pay close attention to what she's saying, and when he *does* speak up his answers are very thoughtful."

Mr. Conner shook his head. "Yes, but the kid has to have a little *life* in him! When I was his age, I was running around like crazy, playing sports, having a great time."

"But Dennis is not you, and he *is* having a great time," replied Mrs. Conner. "He loves designing games and programs on that computer. His science project has a very good chance of winning first place."

Mr. Conner paused. "Maybe I'm not giving him enough credit for what he does well. But I still wish he would get out and *do* more."

"Why don't we ask him to suggest a few places he'd like to go?" suggested Mrs. Conner. "I know they might not be the kind of activities you and I would choose, but if Dennis is willing to get out and be more active, we could go along with it, couldn't we?"

Mr. Conner nodded. "Well, I sure feel out of place at those technology fairs, but maybe Dennis could show me what makes the whole field so appealing to him."

Mrs. Conner smiled. "Why not make your first suggestion an invitation to dinner? Then let's see what develops."

Recognize the Strength

The diligence and perseverance Dennis shows are valuable character traits often missing in the frantic pace of today's society. It is frequently these quiet children, dedicated to a particular task, who will make a significant contribution to our world. These may be among the best of our future scholars and researchers.

Focus on Accountability

As you weigh the time your child spends isolated with the computer against a lack of social involvement, you need to determine if this is a detriment to his or her overall growth and development. If other aspects of the child's life are suffering, such as not getting enough exercise, then some action must be taken. If you approve of all the computer programs and other projects your child is undertaking, your suggestions for relevant activities will probably be all that is needed. Don't forget to appreciate that quiet, thoughtful behavior—some parents would really envy you!

~ 10 ~

Too Much Social Life

"Another birthday party invitation!" exclaimed Bobby's mother. "That makes three just this past month!"

Eight-year-old Bobby beamed. "Yeah, and Susie's having a birthday before Christmas, too!"

Mrs. Jasper frowned. "Bobby, if you paid *half* as much attention to your schoolwork as you do to all your friends, you'd be getting a *lot* better grades."

Bobby shrugged. "Mom, friends are more important than those stupid math problems. School would be way too boring if it wasn't for the parties!"

Mrs. Jasper fought back the urge to do what many of her friends and family members advised her to do. Almost everyone had been counseling her to simply forbid Bobby's spending any more time with his friends until his grades improved. But looking down at his shining face, she realized that Bobby needed those friends as much as they evidently counted on him. If she took away what he did best, would he be motivated to do *anything?* She sighed.

"Bobby, I know that being with your friends is important to you. But your grades are getting worse, and I really need you to concentrate on getting your work done. If I let you invite just one friend over after school tomorrow, which friend would be the best one to help you with your math homework?"

Bobby thought for a moment. "Nancy's really good in math," he admitted. "But she's not very fun. And she's a *girl.* I don't know if she'd want to help me."

Mrs. Jasper put her arm around Bobby. "Maybe she'd come over if she knew you really wanted her to help you by doing what she does best. Then, after you finish your work, you and Nancy could do what *you* do best. Play! You could go roller blading or bicycle riding."

Bobby knew this could be his only chance to combine friends and schoolwork. "OK, Mom. I'll ask Nancy. But next time, can I invite Richard over if we promise to work on our science project?"

Mrs. Jasper smiled and gave Bobby a quick hug. "OK, sport, we'll see how it goes."

Recognize the Strength

Having a friendly, amiable personality can really help a child get along with the multitudes of people that will touch his or her life. It is a gift to be able to interact well with others, and many careers are dependent upon a person's ability to empathize and cooperate with all kinds of people.

Focus on Accountability

If you have a very social child, don't spend too much time trying to substitute academics for social interaction. Concentrate instead on how to productively *combine* the two. Mrs. Jasper recognized that Bobby was much more likely to do his homework if he had a study partner. If you have a child who thrives when working or playing with friends, keep experimenting with ways to get the work done that involves others.

～ 11 ～

Pay Attention to the Details

"I have in my hand an almost perfect paper." Mr. Jensen was addressing his ninth-grade English class with a somewhat dramatic flair.

"The person who turned in the assignment has earned an A+ for content and structure." Now he had everyone's attention. "However, I said *almost* perfect because the person who did this assignment failed to add two very significant words to the paper—his or her first and last *name*." As he held up the paper, there was an audible gasp in the back of the room and Karen Hart sheepishly raised her hand.

"That's my paper, Mr. Jensen." She started forward to retrieve the assignment, but her teacher stopped her.

"Karen, let's talk after class—I'll give you the paper at that time."

Karen felt her heart sink. *Oh no*, she thought, *he's going to give me a zero because I forgot my name again!* She struggled to pay attention during the last half of class and hurried up to Mr. Jensen's desk right after the bell rang.

"Karen, this is yet another in a pattern of careless mistakes you have made during the first few weeks of school," Mr. Jensen began. Karen's face reflected her dismay, and Mr. Jensen hurried on. "Now, Karen, you and I both know that you are gifted when it comes to the written word. I personally believe you are capable of great achievements as a writer or journalist. But they can't send the checks to a person who hasn't identified herself as the author."

Karen nodded. "I know, Mr. Jensen. I'm really sorry. I just get in a hurry to get done, and I forget some of the details." She paused a moment. "Do you really think I could become a *writer?*"

Mr. Jensen smiled. He truly wanted to encourage her, but how could he impress upon her the importance of getting the details right?

"Karen, your ability to hurry and finish a writing assignment quickly is and will be a great asset when you are up against an immovable deadline. But if what you write lacks accuracy, in many cases it would be better that you never hand it in at all. You could be sued; you could lose your job—you could even ruin your whole career."

Karen looked at him soberly. "Mr. Jensen, I *do* want to be a writer. And I want to be a great one. What should I do?"

Mr. Jensen picked up a pencil and clean sheet of paper. "I'll tell you what. If you're serious about this, I'll be more like your editor than your teacher. I'll hold you to the same standards in your writing that an experienced editor at the City Desk would. But every time you make an important error, every time you forget a significant detail or compromise accuracy, I'll keep track of what it might have cost you had you actually been on the job."

"OK," Karen replied eagerly.

Mr. Jensen made his first entry on the paper. "You won't be paid for this article you handed in yesterday. As a matter of fact, because it went in authored by 'anonymous,' virtually anyone could step forward and take the credit for it. Hmm, too bad. I think this could be an award-winning piece."

Karen frowned. "I don't think that's fair, Mr. Jensen. You *know* I wrote it." She could tell by Mr. Jensen's face that she wasn't going to win this battle.

"Karen, are you sure you're ready to *work* for me?" he asked seriously. She grinned and stood up straighter.

"Absolutely," she replied.

"Then start calling me *Boss*," Mr. Jensen told her, "and spend your time working on the next award-winning assignment instead of whining about what went wrong with this one."

Karen quickly gathered her papers and gave Mr. Jensen one last glance.

"You're not going to have to write much on that piece of paper, *Boss*," she told him, nodding toward the tally he had begun. He shrugged and smiled.

"Prove it, Karen," he said quietly.

Recognize the Strength

For children like Karen, determination and earnestness can help them set very high goals and then work diligently to reach them. Karen's sense of the bigger picture and enthusiasm for writing down her ideas will be real assets to her later on in her work life.

Focus on Accountability

Helping your child focus on details, like making sure to put a name on the paper, is important. It will be easy for some to remember and hard for others, no matter what tricks or gimmicks are tried. Helping children see how attention to detail fits into the bigger picture of career success, and how it may eventually affect their pocketbook, may help them realize that details are important. Having a teacher take a personal interest in the child's potential will also go a long way toward keeping the student on track and accountable.

∼ 12 ∼
Who's That Tap-Tap-Tapping at My Door?

"There's that noise again!" Mr. Parker had just sat down for a rare family dinner. His wife nodded and passed the rolls.

"Try not to think about it, dear," she said. "It's just Tommy. Since we won't buy him a drum set, he's figured out how to turn almost *anything* into a rhythm-making device!"

Twelve-year-old Sara made a face. Her younger brother was such a *pain!* He was always making some sort of noise or moving things around or tapping on *something.*

Tommy entered the room and took his place at the table. He was breathless. He tapped his fingers on the table and asked for a glass of milk. His mother gave him a warning look, and he quickly addressed his dad.

"Sorry I'm late," he said. "I was doing my homework." Mr. Parker sighed. How could one nine-year-old boy have so much energy? His son was one big bundle of constant rhythm and movement.

"Are you sure you managed to sit still long enough to finish that homework?" Dad asked. He couldn't imagine what Tommy's paper must look like if he moved this much while he wrote.

Tommy shrugged and tapped his feet under the table.

"Stop shaking the table!" Sara cried. "You're *moving* everything!"

Tommy began to protest until he looked down and saw that his feet were, indeed, moving.

"Sorry," he mumbled.

Mr. Parker leaned toward Tommy.

"Son, you're driving your sister crazy with all the noise and movement. As a matter of fact, it pretty much bothers *all* of us when you

49

keep constantly tapping and making sounds while we're trying to concentrate and enjoy a little quiet time."

"Dad," Tommy objected, "I'm just *thinking*! I'm not trying to bug you!"

Mr. Parker thought for a moment. "Tommy, what if we could figure out a way for you to earn that drum set you want?"

Tommy's eyes lit up and he grinned. "Wow, yeah!"

"I'm willing to make a deal with you," his dad began. "I'll buy you a set of drumsticks first, and you can use them to tap on anything in the house that won't make a noise others can hear and won't hurt the object you're tapping—something like your mattress. If you can go a whole week without causing your sister, your mother, or me, to complain about noise or disruption, I'll begin putting five dollars a week into the fund for your drum set. If you keep up with your schoolwork and maintain some peace and quiet around here, I'll keep contributing to the fund until we have enough to buy the drums."

Tommy's eyes were shining, and his whole leg was shaking under the table. "Wow! No problem! I'll do it!" he cried.

Mrs. Parker excused herself for a moment and brought back a large empty pin cushion and a pencil. "Tommy," she said, "why not try tapping on this?"

As they continued to eat, Tommy happily and silently tapped his pencil on the pin cushion with his left hand while he ate with his right hand. At one point, Sara complained about being distracted by the movement, but Dad suggested she sit where she couldn't *see* Tommy's hand. After all, he reminded her, Tommy *was* doing what he had been asked to do (in this case, eat dinner), and they weren't going to argue about the details.

As Mr. Parker helped his wife clear the table, he strained to hear Tommy up in his room. When no sounds drifted downstairs, he shook his head. "You know, it's almost *too* quiet," he commented to his wife.

Recognize the Strength

This child is kinesthetic (needs to move) and learns while moving. In fact, he almost must move in order to learn. To do what he does best, he needs to keep moving! His energy level is high and needs to be directed in creative and acceptable ways.

Focus on Accountability

Helping your child recognize and understand that noise and movement can irritate and distract others from concentrating may be the most important step. Once you've raised the child's awareness, help by suggesting some appropriate and acceptable ways to move without frustrating others. For these very active children, focusing their energy toward a variety of seasonal sports—or, as in this case, music—may also help them excel in a new energy-filled activity they have not tried before.

~ 13 ~

Why Do You Take Things So Personally?

Rhonda Baker was walking slowly and sadly from her first-grade classroom to the line of cars waiting in the loading zone in front of the school. Mrs. Baker looked concerned as she got out of the car to hurry the petite redhead into the front seat. Rhonda had barely put on her seat belt before the tears spilled onto her cheeks.

"Oh, Rhonda, what is it?" her mother asked. The car behind them honked and Mrs. Baker hurried to pull out onto the street. Rhonda was sobbing quietly now, and her mom felt a sense of helplessness as she guided the car down the busy street. Her daughter had always been an extremely sensitive child. Things had been going very well during the opening weeks of first grade, and she had assumed everything was going to be all right.

Rhonda adored her teacher, Mrs. Black, and she was usually bubbling over with a happy retelling of her day the moment she got into the car after school. Now she only shook her head silently and kept crying.

Mrs. Baker pulled the car into the garage and put her arm around Rhonda.

"Sweetheart, Daddy's home early today. Why don't we go in and get some milk and pretzels and you can tell us what has upset you so much?"

Without saying anything, Rhonda complied. She slowly gathered her books and walked into the kitchen. Mr. Baker was doing paperwork at the kitchen table, and looked up when they came in.

"Wow! I've never seen a first-grader that looked any sadder than you, princess! Did you just lose your best friend?"

Rhonda frowned and Mrs. Baker cast him a warning look.

"Oops—sorry. I forgot we don't kid about things like that." He reached over and gave Rhonda a small squeeze.

Mrs. Baker put the milk and pretzels in front of Rhonda and sat down.

"OK, honey, tell us what happened."

Rhonda burst into fresh tears and struggled to get the words out. "Mrs. Black...she used to like me...and...now she *hates* me!"

"Oh, sweetie, I'm sure that's not true!" exclaimed her mother. "Why would you even *think* that?"

Rhonda took the tissue her mother offered and wiped her nose. "Because she...she put...she put my *name* on the board!"

Mr. Baker looked a little exasperated. "Oh, for heaven's sake, Rhonda, that's no big deal. Boy, if I had a nickel for every time *my* name ended up on the blackboard...." His wife was frowning at him.

"No, Daddy, you don't *understand!* Only the *bad* kids get their names written on the board! I *never* thought Mrs. Black would think I was a *bad* kid!"

Rhonda's parents exchanged glances. They were used to Rhonda overreacting emotionally, but this time she seemed truly devastated. Her dad spoke first. "Rhonda," he said calmly, "start at the beginning. Why did Mrs. Black write your name on the board?"

Rhonda hesitated. "Well, I think I was talking too much to Michelle."

Mr. Baker nodded. "Did Michelle get her name written on the board, too?" he asked. Rhonda nodded.

Mrs. Baker reached over and took Rhonda's hand. "Sweetheart, you must have forgotten how important it is to listen when your teacher talks in class." Then a thought occurred to her. "Rhonda, were there any other names on the board besides yours and Michelle's?"

Rhonda nodded again. Her dad leaned forward. "How many names were on the board, Rhonda?"

She thought for a moment. "Twenty-four, I think," she said somberly.

Her dad struggled not to lose patience. "Rhonda, that's how many kids you have in your whole class. Did the whole class get their names written on the board?"

Rhonda shrugged and said, "I think so." Mrs. Baker put her arm around Rhonda's shoulders.

"Honey, do you think maybe Mrs. Black was having a rough day? It sounds to me like all the kids were giving her a hard time. I'll bet most of them were like you—they didn't realize how much they were misbehaving. Maybe the only way Mrs. Black could get everybody's attention and let them know she was really serious was to write their names on the board."

Rhonda seemed to consider this possibility for the first time. Her face brightened. "Mommy, do you think she still likes me, then?"

Her dad grinned. "Rhonda, I *guarantee* she still likes you."

Mrs. Baker stood to her feet. "Rhonda, if Mrs. Black had a bad day, why don't we bake her some of your favorite cookies and give them to her tomorrow?"

Rhonda leaped to her feet. "Oh yes! And I'll draw her a nice picture to tell her I'm sorry for talking to Michelle and making her have a bad day." As she darted into the other room to gather her drawing paper and pens, Mr. and Mrs. Baker smiled at each other.

"Guess it's just a matter of getting the right perspective," Mr. Baker mused. His wife nodded.

"I just didn't realize how hard it would be to raise such a sensitive, lovable kid!" she sighed.

Recognize the Strength

A child who is sensitive and caring about other people's feelings will grow into an adult who will intuitively be able to understand friends and coworkers with a greater degree of compassion and empathy.

Focus on Accountability

It is important to talk patiently with your child and sort through emotions that are out of control. You need to get down to the facts of what happened and put the whole incident into perspective. When your child is very sensitive, it is important not to diminish his or her feelings, but to try to help the child work with those feelings to solve the problem. As he or she grows older, your child will have a deeper sensitivity to the needs of others and will be valued as a sincere friend.

～ 14 ～

You Can't Make Me

Mrs. Rogers waited patiently to take Shannon home after basketball practice. She felt a sense of pride when she thought about her daughter's future. With only one semester of high school left, Shannon had next year pretty well planned. Her first choice of universities had not only accepted her, but had given her a generous scholarship in basketball and academics. These past three years of private school had certainly been worthwhile, even though they had been very expensive.

"Hi, Mom!" Shannon startled her mother as she energetically burst into the car, pulling her jacket, books, and ever-present basketball into the front seat.

Mrs. Rogers smiled. *What a great kid!* "Hi, honey," she replied. "Did you have a good day?"

Shannon hesitated before replying. "Well, it was OK. I need to talk to you and Dad about something tonight, though."

Mrs. Rogers looked worried. It wasn't like Shannon to arrange a family meeting in advance. Even though her daughter was trying to sound casual, she knew something was up.

After dinner, Mom, Dad, and Shannon remained at the table, and Shannon told her story. It had happened in Language Arts class. Mr. Smith was a teacher with very traditional methods and, according to Shannon, had very "old-fashioned" ideas when it came to discipline and classroom management. Shannon had been practicing with her basketball during lunch and hadn't taken time to drop the ball off at her locker before racing to Mr. Smith's class. As it turned out, Mr. Smith himself was late, so Shannon slipped unnoticed into her seat in the back of the classroom.

Because she was naturally restless and energetic, Shannon continued to dribble the basketball while waiting for Mr. Smith, using the wall and the floor for bouncing surfaces. She became so absorbed in her activity she didn't notice that Mr. Smith had returned and was waiting for everyone's attention. Her reverie broke when she heard him make a loud and angry announcement. "Will the person who is bouncing the basketball kindly identify herself?"

Shannon quickly stopped bouncing and hurriedly stuffed the ball under her seat. Mr. Smith was glaring at her.

"Miss Rogers, do you think it is appropriate to play basketball in Language Arts class?"

Shannon shrugged. "Sorry, Mr. Smith."

"Shannon, I asked you a *question*. Do you believe your behavior was appropriate?"

Shannon was beginning to feel defensive. What was the big deal? After all, she quit as soon as he told her to stop. Wasn't the answer to the question pretty obvious? Mr. Smith was waiting for her response.

Shannon shrugged again and answered quietly, "I don't know."

It didn't take long to figure out that her answer was *not* the one Mr. Smith was looking for. His face was turning red, and he set his textbook down on his desk with a loud *whump!*

"Miss Rogers, you will write an essay for me on the following topic: *Why it is not appropriate to play basketball in Language Arts class.* This essay will be three hundred to five hundred words and will be due Friday. Is that clear?"

Shannon was taken off guard. Whoa, what was happening here? She began to protest.

"Mr. Smith, I..."

"Miss Rogers, you have already wasted enough of our time. If you have any questions, you may see me after class."

Shannon's dad was listening carefully, and looked at her closely. He knew his daughter very well, and although she was usually cooperative, she *did* have a good-sized stubborn streak.

"Shannon, have you started writing the essay?" he asked her, dreading the answer.

"Dad," she replied. "It's a *stupid* assignment. I'm not going to waste my time writing some dumb essay."

Mrs. Rogers looked concerned. "But Shannon, have you thought about the consequences?"

Shannon looked disgusted. "Oh, Mom, what can he do? So I get a zero. Big deal. It's not like he's going to *flunk* me or anything."

Both parents exchanged glances. They had agreed long ago that Shannon needed to take responsibility for her own decisions. This might be a tough one, but they needed to let *her* decide.

Friday came and went, and Shannon did not turn in the essay. Instead of simply receiving a zero, she received an ultimatum. Mr. Smith contacted Shannon and her parents. Shannon's refusal to turn in the essay would be treated as insubordination, and she would not be admitted back into class until the essay was completed, he told them. "Furthermore," Mr. Smith informed them, "this Language Arts credit is necessary for Shannon's graduation. She will not be receiving a diploma unless she completes the requirement."

Mrs. Rogers was frantic. Did Shannon realize what was hanging in the balance? Was this worth sacrificing the scholarship? The tuition? The well-laid plans?

Shannon stood firm. "Mom," she explained, "this is ridiculous. It's an unfair punishment. I'm not going to do it. If I have to wait to go to college, I will."

Dad couldn't contain himself. "Shannon, I think you're being very unwise to make this an issue. Mr. Smith has made himself very clear, and now he can't back down without looking like he gave in to your disobedience. I respect your opinion about this, but I want you to figure out how to salvage your senior year and go on with the rest of your life."

Shannon looked frustrated, but nodded and went to her room. An hour or so later, Mom passed her doorway and peeked in. Shannon had papers spread out on the floor. She was typing furiously on her computer. Mom approached her cautiously.

"Shannon, are you writing the essay?" she asked. Shannon looked up at her.

"Well, I'm writing *an* essay. But I'm not going to write about the dumb topic Mr. Smith wants. I'm writing about what I want to do with my future, and why bouncing a basketball is important to my plans."

Mr. and Mrs. Rogers breathed a sigh of relief the next day when Shannon reported that Mr. Smith had accepted the essay, along with her apology for irritating him by bouncing the basketball.

Recognize the Strength

A determined spirit needs to be directed down a positive road, because such determination can be a driving force toward accomplishing higher and more powerful goals.

Focus on Accountability

Standing firm on one's convictions can lead others to admire your strength of character. But sometimes, as in Shannon's case, it can also cause others to view you as insubordinate and disrespectful. Helping your child climb into the other person's shoes, to view the circumstances from that perspective, and to be held accountable for bottom-line behavior is critical. If your child tends to react like Shannon, helping him or her see both sides, take responsibility for the original behavior, and work through the choices to reach an acceptable outcome will be perhaps the most demanding job you have. As Mr. and Mrs. Rogers discovered later on, the resoluteness of their daughter about the essay would be the same resoluteness that would make her a success in college and in life.

～ 15 ～

It Takes Him Forever to Do Anything

Brandon's mother was in a hurry when she dropped him off at the children's session for Wednesday night church. She gave him a gentle nudge into the room and spoke to Mrs. Sampson, the head teacher.

"Wouldn't you think a five year old could move just a little *faster* than this?"

Mrs. Sampson smiled. "I *have* noticed that Brandon likes to take his time doing almost *everything*," she admitted. "But he sure does some fine work when it comes to his crafts and worksheets. We love watching him work—he's so careful to do everything just right!"

The newest teaching assistant, Susan Barker, approached Mrs. Sampson.

"Time to get started!" she said cheerfully. "We've got a lot to accomplish this hour. I've got six different activities planned so the children can keep moving and do a whole variety of fun things."

Mrs. Sampson smiled knowingly. "Susan," she reminded her. "Don't be surprised if some of the children don't move quite that quickly." Susan looked surprised. *After all,* she thought, *kids have such a short attention span—shouldn't they respond best to lots of quick activities?*

As the children began their first ten-minute activity—the paper plate collage—Susan noticed that Brandon was very carefully cutting each construction paper strip exactly the same size. She glanced at her watch and warned the kids that there were only a couple of minutes left before the puppet show. Although many children were ready to drop what they were doing and get a front seat for the puppet show, Brandon appeared totally unaffected by the announcement. Susan put her arm around him.

"Brandon, it's time to put this stuff away and go to your seat for the puppet show." He ignored her and continued his careful placement of colored strips on the paper plate. Just as the puppet show began, Susan tried again. "Brandon," she explained patiently, "you're going to miss the puppet show. Let's put this away and go over to the puppet corner." Brandon frowned and shook his head.

"I'm not finished," he said simply.

Susan was beginning to lose her patience. All the other children were waiting for the puppets. "Brandon, for heaven's sake, just stick these strips on here. Let's go to the puppet show."

Brandon looked hurt. Mrs. Sampson stepped in and put her hand on Susan's arm.

"Mrs. Barker, why don't you go ahead and start the puppet show without us? I'd like to see what Brandon has planned for this paper plate collage. I sure like what he's done so far."

Three ten-minute activities later, Mrs. Wilson and Brandon proudly showed Mrs. Barker the paper plate collage. Susan shook her head in amazement as Brandon finally walked over to another activity center.

"Why did it take him so *long* to do one simple thing?" she asked.

Mrs. Sampson shrugged. "You know, his mom wants to know that, too. But I think maybe we're all just insisting that Brandon do everything on *our* timeline. You have to admit, he did a wonderful job on his collage—it just took him three times as long as you had planned. But what's the point? He was happily engaged in doing a productive task, and he's pleased with the results."

Susan Barker nodded. "I'm afraid I sometimes forget that not every child moves as quickly as I expect them to. I'm going to really make an effort to help some of these kids by slowing down!"

Mrs. Sampson looked over at Brandon, who was contentedly drawing a deliberate and meticulous line through a scripture maze. "Now if only we could convince his mother to do the same thing!" she mused.

Recognize the Strength

Deliberate, well-thought-out actions are worth their weight in gold in our hurry-up, drive-through world. Appreciate and value the accurate work these children do, without over-emphasizing the speed with which it was done.

Focus on Accountability

Children like Brandon constantly feel pushed to do more, work faster, run further. In a society that values quickness, timing our movements in micro-seconds, children like this may always feel out of sync with their peers. It is quite possible that every job these children undertake in their lifetimes will be a job labeled "Well done." As long as we don't just focus on speed and quantity, but rather on the *quality* of work, children like this will be valued as diligent and thorough workers.

~ 16 ~

Do You Have to Play All the Time?

Helen felt frustration threatening to overwhelm her as she led her four-year-old son Patrick through airport security. How could he be so exuberant this early in the morning? She shifted her bags so they could lie flat on the X-ray machine and followed her energetic son through the doorway.

"Patrick, stand still," she instructed him. "Let's get our stuff." But Patrick was already talking to one of the security officers, playing the "guess which hand it's in" game. Helen apologized to the smiling man in uniform and pulled Patrick away.

"Mommy!" he objected. "I was just playing!"

Helen frowned at him. "Patrick, we don't have time to play—we need to go find our airplane. Don't you want to go see Grandma?"

His young face brightened. "Yes! Grandma has *lots* of stuff to play with!"

Helen took his hand and kept pulling him toward the departure gate.

"Mommy, look!" Patrick was pointing to a brightly colored display window at the gift shop. He pressed his nose to the glass and studied the array of toys and games.

"Wow!" he exclaimed. "Look at all the toys! Can I have one, Mommy? Please?"

"No, Patrick. I told you, we are trying to catch an airplane and go see Grandma. We are *not* shopping for toys."

Patrick looked disappointed for a moment, then smiled again.

"I want to look at these toys, Mommy. Can I just *look* at them?"

"Patrick, NO! Now let's go. There will be time to play later." Helen took her son's arm and continued down the hall. Fortunately, their departure gate wasn't far. Helen glanced at the check-in counter and noted that they wouldn't be boarding for at least another twenty minutes. *Great,* she thought grimly. *Now I'll have to get Patrick to sit still for more than five minutes.* He had already disappeared.

"Patrick? Where are you?" Helen fought momentary panic.

"Here, Mommy!" he replied cheerfully, as he crawled out from under the row of seats. "I'm playing hide and seek!"

"Patrick, get up here and *sit down.* I mean it." She pointed to the seat next to her, and look apologetically at the older woman who was sitting in the seat above Patrick's hiding place.

"I'm sorry," Helen said to her. "All he thinks about is play, play, play." The older woman smiled.

"He's about four, isn't he?" she asked Helen. Helen nodded. "Well, he's certainly a healthy, well-balanced child, then," she commented. "Children don't play enough these days."

Helen shook her head. "Oh, Patrick doesn't have *that* problem. He wants to play *too much.* I can't get him to sit still for more than a minute or two." Patrick was walking down the row of chairs toward a man who was reading a book. Helen knew she had to head him off before he tried to engage another playmate.

"Patrick! Come back here this instant!" As he reluctantly returned to his mother, the older woman nodded wisely.

"Children like Patrick are certainly exhausting," she said to Helen. Helen quickly agreed while she picked her son up and sat him in the chair beside her. The older woman continued.

"Patrick has a wonderful sense of warmth and playfulness. He sure seems to make friends easily."

"That's for sure," Helen replied. "He's going to get in trouble if he doesn't settle down and stick with me."

The older woman hesitated and then spoke. "I know it's not my place," she began. "But if you don't mind my saying so, Patrick just wants to spend time with those who will play with him, because he wants to share his favorite activity with those he loves. Frankly, I'm complimented that he chose me to be one of his new friends."

Helen watched Patrick squirming in his seat as he scanned the group waiting in the airport. Suddenly she realized how small and vulnerable this bundle of energy really was. She wanted so much to hold him close, but he would never sit still long enough! *I know why he's always trying to get away from me,* she thought. *I don't make a very good playmate. I'm always trying to get him to stop having fun.* She glanced at some of the other adults waiting. *The last thing I want is for him to turn to a stranger. One of his favorite people to play with should be me,* she admitted to herself.

"Patrick," she said. He turned quickly and looked at her expectantly.

"Patrick, which hand do you think I have the candy in?" His face was beaming as he enthusiastically entered the contest. The older woman across from them was smiling warmly.

"He's a great kid," she told Helen. Helen nodded.

"Thanks for reminding me," she replied.

Recognize the Strength

Children like Patrick with a natural sense of playfulness, spontaneity, and warmth bring energy and light to a world so often dark and serious. Instead of trying to still the voice and calm the spirit, why not enjoy a sense of appreciation for the pure joy of childhood?

Focus on Accountability

Obviously, parents must convey a sense of responsibility to their children. But when they are very young, they also need to preserve a spirit of joyful participation in youth. Provide safety and structure, but allow your child to be a child as much as possible. If your child's favorite person to be with isn't you, who will it be?

~ 17 ~

Do You Want to Go to School Naked?

Stella was a dedicated single mom with a very determined nine year old—Hank. She had read books and taken several seminars about the strong-willed child. So far she had been pretty successful with the techniques she had learned and practiced on Hank. But she experienced a critical test one fateful Monday morning.

Hank attended a private, conservative school. Stella felt certain that this school was the best place to meet his individual needs. Hank had complained about the uniforms at first, but so far he had worn them without argument. Perhaps he got up on "the wrong side of the bed" that Monday. Maybe he didn't get quite enough sleep. Or maybe the compliant side of his nature was simply used up. For whatever reason, Hank decided he was *not* wearing his uniform to school that day. Stella was in a hurry. She had to meet with an important client and didn't have time for much negotiation before work.

It was ten minutes before their scheduled departure, and Hank was still completely undressed. Stella was exasperated. "Hank, *get dressed!*"

Hank glared at her. "Mom, I *told* you. I'm not going to wear that stupid uniform!"

Stella heard herself saying the very thing she knew was the worst thing to say. "Hank, you either wear that uniform or you go to school wearing *nothing!* Do you understand?" Hank seemed to consider the possibility for a moment. He couldn't imagine that his quiet, conservative mother would actually carry out such an absurd threat. He stood to his full height and decided to call his mother's bluff.

"OK, Mom. I'll go to school naked." He watched her face carefully for her reaction. Surely his mother wasn't going to let him walk out of the house *naked*.

Stella was caught off guard momentarily, but quickly recovered.

OK, she told herself, *just stay calm and call his bluff. He's not going to walk out of the house naked.*

"OK," she said, "get on out to the car, then. We've got to go." With only a moment's hesitation, Hank picked up his school books and headed toward the car.

Now Stella fought panic. Her nine-year-old son had just walked out to the car, stark naked, and was prepared to go to school that way. She forced herself to stay calm. She knew how important it was going to be not to betray her emotions. Quickly, she gathered Hank's clothes and took them to the car with her, tossing the pile casually into the back seat.

As she drove to school, her mind was racing. *What if he really goes through with this? Should I back down and keep him from being humiliated?*

Hank's mind was busy with similar thoughts. *Would Mom actually let me get out of the car naked? What have I gotten myself into?*

They reached the last stop sign before the turn into the driveway of the school. Stella took a deep breath and turned on the right turn signal. As she negotiated the corner, Hank suddenly leaped into the back seat and pulled on his clothes. In a matter of seconds, he was poised to get out of the car and join the kids scurrying into their classrooms. Without saying a word, Stella reached over and kissed him on the cheek. He gave her a quick wave and took off for yet another ordinary day of school.

Anyone who asks Stella about that day immediately sees a smile appear on her face. "You know," she says, "to this day Hank is not really sure if I would have *actually* let him get out of that car. There's a real healthy sense of respect between us." Would she want to live through that morning again?

"Never!"

Recognize the Strength

Hank's strength is that when he makes up his mind that something is really important to him, he stands by his decision, no matter what. In this case, his youth and immaturity could certainly have caused him and his mother embarrassment. But when the strength is developed, Hank will be a man who stands by his convictions—do or die.

Focus on Accountability

Calling a bluff is a dangerous game to play. You must use great caution and be willing to accept the consequences, whatever they may be. In this case, both Hank and Stella each had a set of choices.

Hank had two options: going to school naked or going to school wearing his uniform. Stella also had two options: delivering Hank on time and naked or delivering Hank on time and dressed in his uniform. Stella showed a lot of restraint and wisdom by refusing to make a big deal out of Hank's bold move to call her bluff. By responding calmly and showing no surprise when Hank went ahead and pulled on his clothes, she let *both* of them experience victory.

∼ 18 ∼

Gotta Move

"Renee! Come tell Grandma what you memorized in school today!" Complying with her mother's request, five-year-old Renee Stevens bounded down the stairs eagerly and almost knocked her grandmother down with an enthusiastic hug.

"Grandma! I learned the *whole* Lord's Prayer!" Renee's face was shining, and she was practically dancing. Grandma struggled to maintain her balance as the small bundle of energy pulled her over to the sofa.

"Sit down, Mommy and Grandma, and I'll *tell* it to you!"

While the two adults sat down to listen, Renee began pacing across the entire living room floor, reciting the text perfectly. Grandma called to her.

"Renee, sweetheart, come stand here and look at me. We can't hear what you're saying when you're walking back and forth."

Renee reluctantly walked toward her grandma and stood in front of her.

"Renee, that sounded wonderful! Stand right here and tell me again so I can hear every word and see your eyes sparkle."

Renee tried standing still, but couldn't help squirming as she tried to remember what it was she was supposed to be saying.

"Go ahead, honey," her mother was saying. "Do you need me to help you start?"

Renee frowned. This didn't seem like much fun anymore. She glanced out the window and noticed her friend Sally and Sally's mom playing in the yard next door.

"I want to go play with Sally!" she declared, and began to run out the front door.

"Renee!" her mother called to her. "Come back and finish what you were doing!" Renee stopped in her tracks and turned to her mom.

"I don't remember," she stated truthfully. "Can I go now?"

Her mother sighed and nodded. "Stay where I can see you," she reminded Renee. She was gone in a flash.

Grandma Stevens looked concerned. "Carol, when is that child going to learn to be still?" she asked her daughter-in-law. Carol shook her head.

"Mom, I don't think she really *can* be very still. She's in constant motion. The teacher at her private Christian school has already sent home two notes in the first three weeks of school warning me that Renee has trouble sitting still and paying attention in class. But the thing is, Renee's very bright. She has memorized significant portions of text and she's already reading some words. It's just that she can't seem to remember anything unless she can walk around or move while she's doing it."

Grandma Stevens frowned. "Well, she's going to have to learn that sitting still is very important. You may need to be a little harder on her."

Carol smiled at her mother-in-law. "Mom, no offense, but I don't think it's nearly as important for Renee to be still as it is for her to enjoy learning. I'm trying to work with her teacher to figure out ways we can combine Renee's love of learning with her need to keep moving." She sighed. "I have to admit—it's a real challenge."

Grandma Stevens stood up and stretched. "Well, I'll certainly admit that Renee did a wonderful job of memorizing the Lord's Prayer. I hope you can get her to slow down a little and think about what she's saying."

Carol grinned. "Mom, I really believe the only way Renee *can* think about what she's saying is to *speed up—and keep moving!*"

Recognize the Strength

A child's energy and enthusiasm for learning will often be the key to committing information to memory. Encouraging the natural inclination to keep moving while learning or remembering information will help your child for years to come.

Focus on Accountability

As adults, it's hard to remember that we need to "lighten up" a bit when we are in a child's world. In this case, the child could easily recite the memorized work while walking around, but not while standing still. Ask yourself an important question: "Do I want him to remember the information, or to stand still?" *What's the point?*

~ 19 ~

Tattletale

"Mom! Quentin's hammering stuff on the wall again! You told him not to, but he's doing it anyway!"

Sharon Jones thought she would explode if her daughter tattled on her twelve-year-old brother one more time.

"Tanya!" she called. "I've had it with your tattling!"

A blonde, perky eight-year-old head peeked around the corner. "But Mom, you *said* Quentin wasn't supposed to…"

Her mom interrupted her. "Tanya, I *mean* it. I'm sick to death of hearing you complain about Quentin. *I'll* be the mother, OK?"

Tanya frowned, and Sharon could tell her daughter was trying to figure out what that last comment meant. Tanya was so literal, so predictable, so *picky* about every little detail. She sighed. Although Tanya was an easy child to live with when it came to keeping things clean and organized, she could really be difficult when everyone else in the family didn't do things her way. *And let's face it,* she thought, *Quentin is almost exactly the opposite of his sister in every way.* Quentin was basically a good kid, she knew. But he would never be as organized or as fastidious as his sister. And his mind simply worked from an entirely different perspective than Tanya's. He was a creative, lovable, free spirit, constantly being watched and evaluated by his by-the-book sister.

How could they ever achieve peace in the family if Tanya wouldn't let Quentin be himself? It seemed like their mom had tried everything to help the two siblings get along. Threats hadn't worked; rewards simply resulted in more arguments about why they both didn't want the same thing. Everything had to be spelled out for Tanya, down to the last detail. Even in third grade, she was already dependent upon lists, preferring that as much as possible be put in writing. Although

Quentin was easy to communicate with simply by talking, Tanya almost always needed something concrete or tangible in her hand before she really understood what was expected of her.

Suddenly Sharon had a great idea. Maybe she could convince Tanya to stop tattling so much if there were some tangible proof that tattling didn't help. The next day, after school, Sharon took Tanya aside and proposed her plan.

"Tanya," her mom began. "I've got an idea for how you and Quentin and I can get along better. I know that you and I often disagree about whether or not what Quentin is doing needs to be reported to me. You know I don't like to hear dozens of tattletales, and I know it bugs you to think your brother is getting away with something he shouldn't do. So here's my idea." Sharon pulled out a large roll of tickets. Tanya recognized them immediately.

"Hey, Mom, these are like the tickets we use to get into plays and concerts and stuff!" Sharon nodded.

"But these are *Tattletale Tickets*," she told her daughter. "I'm going to give you five of these tickets at the beginning of every day. During the day, if you find that you just have to tell on Quentin, you'll need to give up one *Tattletale Ticket* for each time you tattle on him. When you're out of tickets, you're out of tattling until the next day when you start over with five more tickets."

Tanya was frowning. "Why do I only get *five?*" she asked. Her mom smiled.

"Now, Tanya, I think you know that Quentin's not a bad kid. I'll bet you could even get to like him a lot more if you weren't so worried about getting him in trouble. You'll just need to decide which things are really worth giving up a ticket for when it comes to telling on him."

Tanya considered the situation for a moment. "But Mom, if Quentin knows I only have five tickets, he'll make me give them up right away and then do anything he wants!"

Her mom nodded. "I thought of that. This needs to be a secret between you and me, Tanya. Quentin shouldn't know that you and I have this ticket agreement. Let's just give this a try for a week—deal?"

Tanya was thoughtful. "Well, OK."

Sharon breathed a quick sigh of relief. She sure hoped this would work.

Tanya had only been gone a few minutes when Sharon heard her calling.

"Mom! Mom!"

"What is it, Tanya?"

"Quentin is—Oh, never mind."

Sharon smiled. So far, so good!

Recognize the Strength

Tanya appears to have the ability to remember all the details, and hold everyone accountable for them. This will be of great use when working on large projects or when there are many people involved in a project. By limiting her "tattling" to a specific number of tickets, Sharon Jones is helping her daughter make some choices about what is important and why. Someday Tanya will make her mother very proud when she is a great chairperson, an office manager, a planning consultant, or is involved in some endeavor where her organizational skills and memory for detail and accountability will be a great asset.

Focus on Accountability

Tanya irritated those around her by tattling about virtually everything. Trying to limit the tales was a good exercise in self-discipline for Tanya. By providing a concrete, visible number of tickets, Tanya could begin to monitor her own behavior and decide which battles were really worth fighting. If you have a child like Tanya, give this method a try, or you may want to invent some other creative way for your own "tattletale" to keep a healthy perspective.

~ 20 ~

How Will We Ever Get You Organized?

"Mom! Where's my permission slip?" John was rummaging through a stack of papers he had evidently left on the kitchen counter.

Sally Taylor looked at her teenage son with a mixture of exasperation and resignation.

"John, it is *not* my job to keep track of your things."

John grinned at his mom. "Sorry, Mom—I just start going in too many directions, and I forget where I put stuff."

Sally had to agree with him. She had grown up in a very organized household. Her mother had always insisted there was a place for everything, and everything should be in its place. She had tried so hard to pass this quality on to her children, but John just didn't think in a straight line. Even as a child, he had been so easily distracted that he left at least a dozen toys or games strung over two or three rooms, playing with each one only briefly before moving on to the next point of interest.

When John started school, his lack of organization seemed magnified. He was constantly misplacing his assignments and textbooks. Although he seemed frustrated with himself for not being able to keep track of his possessions, he couldn't seem to concentrate on such minute details. His mind thought in such broad, imaginative pictures that even his best intentions of putting his things in a specific place never happened.

Sally had tried at least a dozen systems for helping John get organized. She smiled, remembering the complex shelving system she had insisted her husband install. She had spent hours carefully labeling each cubbyhole so that there would be a place for every conceivable item John would need to store and retrieve. But instead of providing structure, the whole idea seemed to confuse him. Were the items in alphabetical order? What if he didn't know what to call everything he needed to put away? What if he forgot what he *did* call something so he couldn't find where it was stored? Since he had so many things on his mind, there always seemed to be a huge pile of stuff beside the shelves waiting to be placed into the correct slot. After Sally discovered a forgotten week-old lunch in one cubby, she gave up, put cupboard doors on the front, and turned the shelves into a pantry.

After the cubbyhole system failure, there had been a parade of organization systems, some expensive, some elaborate, but none that had the desired effect. She sighed.

"What's wrong, Mom?" John was looking intently at her. She reached out and patted his arm.

"I was just wondering what in the world I could do to help you keep track of all your stuff," she admitted. "Every place I make a file, you just seem to make a pile."

John brightened. "Hey, maybe that's it!"

John's dad was the last to come home that evening, and when he came through the back door, he tripped over a new object in the hallway. "What in the world is *that?*" he exclaimed.

"Hi, honey!" Sally said cheerfully. "You just tripped over John's Dump Basket."

"His *what?*"

"Dump Basket." She explained. "John thought of it. He got tired of hearing me complain about how many times he misplaced things, so he went out to the garage and got a big plastic laundry basket. When he gets home each night, he'll just dump everything he brought with him into his basket. If he doesn't have the time or inclination to put things away, he'll at least know where the right pile is in the morning."

"Not a bad idea," her husband said. "The kid's pretty resourceful."

Sally nodded, wondering if there was any way to hide that basket inside the pantry.

Recognize the Strength

John is a kid who's always had a creative mind filled with a variety of thoughts and possibilities. Although organization has not been a priority, John has been successful with school and relationships. His desire to please his mother coupled with his realistic solution demonstrate a real talent for creative problem solving.

Focus on Accountability

John's mother was wise not to make a big deal of what an organizational system looked like as long as it worked. Now she can hold her son accountable for keeping track of his belongings without making him feel frustrated by his lack of attention to the outward appearance of his system.

~ 21 ~

Let's Go Where the Action Is

Richard loved almost everything about his new class. His parents had teased him about being the only teenage boy in his class who was always hoping to run into police officers instead of avoiding them. When the local police department offered preliminary career training for those interested in law enforcement, Richard was the first in line to sign up for the pilot program at his high school.

He had always been interested in being where the action was, and the police training intrigued him. During the first two weeks of class, however, he found that not every cadet shared his enthusiasm for hands-on training. While the instructor talked about various aspects of criminal law, other students were simply taking notes. Richard could barely contain himself. Where could he go to see how this worked? The instructor was patient, but reminded Richard that he needed a little more time to get the paperwork done before he plunged into the hands-on activities.

Richard was eager to visit the police station, the jail, and the morgue. How about field trips? When did all the action start? He did his best to hide his restlessness during lectures, but his sketchy notes reflected his frustration with having to sit still.

After the first major objective test in class, Richard got a rude awakening. His score was barely above passing. He was astonished. This was his favorite class! He *loved* this stuff! How could he flunk out when he was so motivated to succeed?

Richard's dad picked him up from school a couple of days later, and offered to take him out for ice cream. Richard protested.

"Dad, I'm not a little kid anymore."

His dad nodded. "That's for sure! But you still like the same things you always did."

Over their favorite hot fudge sundaes, Richard's dad brought up the subject of his son's new course. Richard looked discouraged.

"Dad, I really thought this would be the best class I've ever taken. I can't believe I'm going to flunk out of something that's so right for me."

Dad shook his head. "Richard, you don't need to flunk out. You just got ahead of yourself. You've always been a kid who just jumped in with both feet, and you don't have much patience for sitting through anything that's not connected to some active task. Your energy and enthusiasm will really be a plus for you, but you've got to balance that with some time to think and process basic information necessary to know how to get the job done."

Richard grimaced. "I know, I know. But I hate just sitting and listening to someone talk!"

His dad smiled. "Richard, if you really want to be a cop, you're going to want others to listen to you when *you* talk. But will you know what to say? Taking field trips and observing others at work can help you figure out how to use information, but if you don't know what you're looking for, all the field trips in the world won't help you recognize it."

Richard nodded. "OK, OK, I get your point. I need to take more notes, listen to more details, get better grades on my tests."

Dad nodded. "I have a feeling the action part isn't very far away. But use your eagerness to see the action as a motivation for learning what to do when they actually turn you loose."

"Got it, Dad." Richard tried to show patience. "Can we go now?"

Recognize the Strength

Richard's determination and enthusiasm can be contagious to others in the police pilot program. Determination, enthusiasm, and hands-on abilities are certainly qualities of leadership. As Richard learns to channel these traits, he can develop his leadership skills and enhance his career choices.

Focus on Accountability

Concrete, hands-on learners like Richard want to use all their senses to learn. They like the action part of learning. For Richard, the lights, the screeching tires, getting the handcuffs on the bad guy, as depicted on TV, all looks very glamorous. But, of course, action is not enough. There has to be book work as well.

Parents and teachers of action-oriented kids need to think about ways to enhance learning by using lots of movement. Perhaps real-life field trips will help illustrate how the foundation of solid knowledge has to be in place before you can jump in and "go with the flow." Try using "what-if" scenarios. Talk through why one course of action would be better than another. Try to make the at-home studying or memorizing as active as possible. Keep reminding your adventurous child that there *will* be fields to conquer—but they need some ammunition and resources.

∼ 22 ∼

Aren't You Finished Yet?

"Andy, do you have your report done?" Mrs. Stone was trying to clear the dining room table of the clutter that surrounded her sixth-grade son. His head was bent in concentration, and he didn't seem to hear her. She leaned closer to his ear.

"Andy, it's almost ten o'clock. You've got to go to bed. Are you done?"

Andy shook his head. "Mom, I don't see how Mr. Maddox expects us to compare the historical version of *Pocahontas* with the Disney animated version. There's more than one historical version, and I haven't even found out how many more actually exist."

Andy's mom looked frustrated. "Andy, this report is due *tomorrow*. You've been working on it for over two weeks. Why don't you just choose one of the historical versions you *have* found and compare that one?"

Andy frowned. "How would I know I chose the right one?" he asked.

Mrs. Stone felt exasperated. "Andy, why does it matter? Did Mr. Maddox tell you to find as many versions as possible?"

Andy shook his head. "But maybe he didn't know there were so many around."

"Andy, you *must* go to bed. You'll just have to ask Mr. Maddox about getting an extension on your deadline at the same time you ask about which historical version of the story he prefers."

She watched the frustration cloud Andy's face and sighed. He'd been like this all his life. He couldn't just take something and run with it. He had to analyze, look at things from every conceivable perspective. He worked so hard on his reports and assignments, and yet he missed so many deadlines while he kept digging for more information.

She just hoped Mr. Maddox would understand. She sat down beside her tired son and pulled the laptop computer over in front of her.

"Andy, why don't we quickly write a note to Mr. Maddox. Let's just describe to him what you've done so far, and why you haven't been able to complete the report on time. You dictate to me, and I'll type. Then Mr. Maddox will at least realize how serious you are about finishing this assignment thoroughly."

Andy smiled. "Gee, Mom, I wish you could be my secretary all the time!"

Recognize the Strength

Thoroughness and diligence are valuable traits. Children like Andy show signs of becoming great researchers, perhaps analyzing and discovering a cure for the common cold, a new medication for the treatment of a major disease, or a solution to civic problems.

Focus on Accountability

Even though Andy is thorough and competent, he is often the victim of analysis-paralysis. Children like Andy often miss deadlines, and their report cards don't reflect their true knowledge and ability. If you are the parent or the teacher of a child like Andy, try to review the assignment individually with him or her before beginning the project. Make sure the child understands what is expected and emphasize that it's not necessary to go beyond that for this particular assignment. Check part way through the project to see if the child is over-analyzing or doing more than is essential to complete the project. This casual monitoring of progress will keep the child focused on the original intent of the project and will hopefully prevent the late-night, last-minute dilemma from occurring.

~ 23 ~

Keep Your Hands Off My Stuff

"Someone get the door!" Susan's mother yelled from the kitchen. Ten-year-old Susan secretly wished no one would get the door. *If we all stay real quiet*, she thought, *maybe they'll just go away*. No such luck, of course. The Mayfields were coming to dinner, and that was that. And her mother always expected her to entertain Angela Mayfield. Angela was four years younger than Susan. Because the adults liked some time to talk among themselves, she was supposed to keep Angela busy. But surely her mother wouldn't expect this if she really knew what kind of trouble Angela caused.

Angela Mayfield was like a human tornado, Susan decided. From the moment she walked in the door to the greatly anticipated moment of her departure, she touched or knocked over practically everything she could reach. "What's this? How does *this* work? Where does this cord *go?* What happens if I push *this* button?" Angela was full of questions, but she never waited for the answer. She just grabbed and tried *everything*.

Susan took one last look at her room before her dad opened the door to let the Mayfields inside. She hoped she had successfully hidden everything breakable. She took a deep breath and went out to meet the walking disaster.

"Hi, Susan!" Angela's voice sounded loud and obnoxious to Susan, but she managed to smile at her. Angela was crossing the room to greet her, touching every piece of furniture as she walked. *Oh no! Here we go again!*

Susan gritted her teeth and started walking toward Angela. Suddenly Susan's mom called out to them.

"Girls, I have something I'd like for you to do."

Angela and Susan both looked at Susan's mom in surprise. What was she talking about?

She dragged a huge box out from behind the big chair in the living room. It was filled with a large assortment of toys, both new and old.

Susan's mom handed both girls a pile of removable stickers and a pen.

"These are toys that need to be sorted and packaged for the homeless children's toy drive coming up next month. I wonder if you girls would go through and decide which toys work, whether all the pieces are there, and for what age the toy would be appropriate."

Susan was astonished. Where had her mom gotten these toys? When did she decide to *do* this? But Angela's eyes were shining, and she had already reached in and pulled out two or three toys.

"Wow! This will be great fun! I used to have one of these! Does this button make the lights go on?"

Susan's mom was helping them drag the box into the family room, smiling at the expression on Susan's face.

"This should take a while," her mom whispered with a wink. "You may never get a chance to play with the stuff in your room."

Susan grinned at her. She didn't know how her mom knew, but she had never been so happy to have a hands-on, time-consuming, tedious job to do!

Recognize the Strength

Angela has a zest for life that at her young age is displayed by touching everything. She, like many children, has an active, eager, inquisitive mind that freely seeks new information from all those around her.

Focus on Accountability

Keeping an active, curious child busy can be a demanding job. A child like Angela learns by touching. Her learning needs to involve active whole body motions. Because Angela's motor skills are not mature yet, she tends to damage many things she touches. It was very wise of Susan to plan ahead and put away those items she cherished.

It was also wise for Susan's mom to plan ahead and provide an unexpected basket of toys to keep all the hands busy.

If you have children like Angela, providing a lot of big-motion, learning activities may be the best way to teach them. Providing multiple learning centers and a list of projects for these children from which they can pick and choose, will be most helpful as their need for hands-on learning moves them through life. Keeping an active, inquisitive mind filled with choices will foster in the child a desire to continue learning.

～ 24 ～

Don't Be So Competitive

"I won! I won!" Jonathan Richards raced into the kitchen, startling his mother. His hair was tousled, his ten-year-old face was shining.

"Mom—I *creamed* them! It was *so* cool! You shoulda seen the other kids just stand there—they didn't even know how to *kick* a soccer ball!"

Mrs. Richards stopped him. "Jonathan, are you talking about soccer practice with your new teammates?"

He snorted. "Team? Man, Mom, I'm the only one who even got the ball into the net. Those wimps don't know how lucky they are that at least *one* of us can score!"

Mrs. Richards frowned. "Jonathan, this is supposed to be a *team* sport. You promised you'd make a real effort to fit into the group this time." Jonathan helped himself to a glass of milk and gave his mother a puzzled look.

"Mom, you want me to do my best, right? I can't help it if I'm the only one who really wants to win."

Mrs. Richards felt her heart sink. They'd been through this before. Jonathan, because of his competitive spirit, had managed to alienate his friends and classmates since kindergarten. He had always wanted to excel, whether it was coming in first in a track meet or taking top honors in a spelling bee. She had tried to help him understand the importance of making friends and accepting others as equals, but even as a small child he had been impatient with anyone who could not keep up with him. Her heart ached as she watched him play and study alone, rarely spending any time at all with friends or classmates.

Jonathan was walking away, hurrying to get on the computer upstairs and write "the best report Mr. Henry has ever read." The telephone was ringing.

"Mrs. Richards?" It was Don Amory, Jonathan's new soccer coach. Mrs. Richards sank into a kitchen chair, dreading what the coach might say.

"Today was the first practice for our soccer team. Jonathan probably told you we had a pretty good scrimmage." The coach continued. "Jonathan has strong athletic ability, Mrs. Richards, and he is certainly a valuable player. But if today is any indication, he's pretty hard on his teammates."

Mrs. Richards sounded apologetic. "Mr. Amory, I don't think he means to be. I'll talk to him, I promise."

"Mrs. Richards, don't take this the wrong way, but do you really think Jonathan is cut out to play team sports? His strong competitive spirit suggests to me that he should be trying out for individual sports, like tennis, swimming, or skiing. He could really excel alone, and he would often be challenging himself to beat his own best record."

Mrs. Richards wasn't sure. "Mr. Amory, are you saying Jonathan shouldn't be on the team?"

"Mrs. Richards, I'm saying that I think Jonathan might make more friends if he wasn't constantly competing with them. I think it's worth at least discussing with him. It might be a relief to you *and* to him."

Mrs. Richards thanked the coach and decided it was worth a try. "Jonathan?" she called. "Would you come down here for a minute, please?"

"In a second, Mom!" he called. "I'm about to beat my own best score on the new computer game!"

She smiled. OK, this might actually work!

Recognize the Strength

The child who is ultra-competitive—who always wants to be on top—will aspire to greatness and being the best at whatever he or she chooses to do in life.

Focus on Accountability

Competition drives kids like Jonathan. The problem is that this kind of child doesn't try to save face or friendships in the battle for top gun. That unrestrained competitive spirit can be tough on relationships with others.

It is important to guide children like this, trying to cushion the effects of their aggressive nature. If they can mold their competitive spirit into leadership qualities, they'll emerge into adulthood as medal-winning athletes, enterprising business owners, or successful entrepreneurs.

How Many Times
Do I Have to Tell You?

Mark was standing in line, waiting to talk to the teacher. It seems like Mrs. Byerly is avoiding looking at me, he thought. Finally, she turned and asked how she could help.

"Mrs. Byerly," he began, "how are we supposed to write answers on the paper? Should we make two columns, or just one?"

Mrs. Byerly looked exasperated. "Mark, I have told the whole class exactly how to do this assignment. Weren't you listening?"

Mark frowned. Was he listening? He knew he hadn't been talking, but he surely didn't remember Mrs. Byerly giving any details about how to write the answers.

"I-I thought I was listening," he replied, "but I guess I didn't hear everything you said."

Mrs. Byerly looked stern. "Well, young man, I think that by the fourth grade you should have learned how to pay attention better than this. You'll just need to ask one of your classmates who was listening." She turned back to a task at her desk.

Mark walked back to his desk, dreading the fact that he would have to ask one of his friends to tell him what he'd evidently missed. Suddenly Mrs. Matthews, the teacher's aide, appeared by his desk.

"Mark, I'll go over the instructions again," she offered. His face brightened. Mrs. Matthews knelt down close to his desk and showed him how to write the answers. His look of relief was evident. She reached over and gave his arm a pat.

"Mark," she said, "I know it's sometimes hard to listen to everything at once. If you're like me, when the teacher gives you instructions, you just want to know what you are supposed to do. You aren't really ready to listen to how to do it."

Mark nodded. How did she know?

Mrs. Matthews went on. "Mark, if you'd like to come in for a while during recess, I'll help you practice listening for details. Then, if you like, I can give your mom some ideas for helping you practice at home, too."

Mark smiled and nodded. "I'd like that, Mrs. Matthews," he said happily.

Later, Mark's mom was relieved when she talked to Mrs. Matthews.

"We've been worried about Mark's attention span," she admitted. "He's such a great kid, and he really seems to grasp information quickly. It's just that he doesn't remember the details later."

Mrs. Matthews smiled. "Well, I haven't had a lot of special training, but I surely have had a lot of experience with this—I'm the same kind of learner. I found that if someone helps me practice listening for details, it really helps. I'd suggest you read aloud to Mark. Give him some details to listen for before you start, and ask him about them when you finish."

Mark's mom nodded. "But what if Mark's teacher doesn't tell him ahead of time what details to listen for?"

Mrs. Matthews nodded. "That's a problem sometimes, but I think if Mark learns to ask the right questions before Mrs. Byerly gets too far into her instructions, he'll be able to get the overall picture of what she's asking him to do. Then he'll be able to listen for the details. I'll help him practice doing that for the next few weeks."

The next day when Mark came to school, he rushed up to his new-found friend. "Thanks, Mrs. Matthews. Now I think I'll live through the fourth grade!"

Recognize the Strength

Mark is the type of child who quickly grasps information, getting the overall picture. He can get the details but he often needs his teacher to understand there are times when he needs the instructions personalized, just as Mrs. Matthews did when she knelt down and explained the directions to him.

Focus on Accountability

Mark, like many children, is a global learner who listens to directions the first time just to get the big picture. They need to know what is happening and where this assignment is taking them. After they get the big picture, they need to hear the directions again to know how to proceed. Although Mark had the "gist" of what was expected, he couldn't focus on the details of how to accomplish the task. If children like Mark are properly challenged and not discouraged by impatient teachers and parents, they can become great interpreters of information and instructions for others. As these children mature they will become strong communicators with a knack for adding those personal touches that facilitate learning.

～ 26 ～

Show a Little Confidence in Yourself

Carla was finished with her test first. She quickly looked around, but none of her eighth-grade classmates appeared to be even close to finishing. Heads bent, they wore expressions that ranged from intense concentration to almost physical pain. Carla frowned. The test hadn't seemed that hard. Was she missing something? Had the teacher simply tricked her into believing she knew the answers? Why had she raced effortlessly through the test while everyone else seemed to take forever? She glanced at the clock. With almost thirty minutes left in class, she would just have to figure out how to look like she was still working on the test. She sure wasn't going to make a fool of herself by walking up there and turning in her grammar test ahead of everyone else.

After English class, Carla walked quickly to math class and took her seat. Mrs. Mather would no doubt have them working problems on the board. *Oh please*, Carla thought, *please don't make me go first!* Mrs. Mather was already talking to the class, but Carla couldn't concentrate on what she was saying. She was fighting the rising feeling of panic that she was about to be called to stand in front of all her classmates and put an answer on the board she wasn't even sure was right.

"Carla? Carla?" Mrs. Mather was calling her name. She looked up. Mrs. Mather was pointing toward the board. "Carla, would you please put the first homework problem on the board?"

Carla felt like she couldn't breathe. When she spoke, her voice was barely above a whisper. "I-I'm sorry, Mrs. Mather. I didn't *do* my homework." There. She'd told a lie, but at least she wouldn't have to look foolish in front of everyone.

Mrs. Mather looked surprised, but decided not to push further. After class, she stopped Carla before she could dash out the door.

"Carla." Mrs. Mather was standing right next to her desk. "Carla, I have never known you not to do your homework. Is something wrong?"

Carla looked miserable. Lying was not something she did well.

"I'm sorry, Mrs. Mather. I just panicked. I didn't want to go to the board. I was afraid my answer wouldn't be right."

Mrs. Mather frowned. "You're one of my best students. Your answers are almost *always* right. I don't understand your reluctance to share your knowledge with the rest of the class."

Carla almost smiled. *Mrs. Mather thinks I'm almost always right!* she thought. *She said I'm one of her best students!*

When she looked at Mrs. Mather, she just shrugged. "I-I guess I'm just afraid everyone will think I'm stupid," she admitted.

Mrs. Mather nodded. "Carla, believe it or not, I understand. You have not yet developed enough confidence in yourself to risk showing everyone else what you know. In many ways, that is a very good thing. You won't be guilty of arrogance or be accused by your friends of being a know-it-all.

"But, Carla," she continued. "You *are* a very bright girl. If you never let others understand that you know what you're doing, they will think you *don't* know the answers. Pretty soon, you may even convince *yourself* that you don't know, and the world will lose a very promising thinker."

Carla nodded. "But I just don't want to go first!" she protested.

Mrs. Mather nodded. "I'll tell you what. At least in *my* class, I'll be sure not to call you up first—but only for the next two weeks. During that time, I want you to check your work, and verify that you know most of the answers. Pretend that you *did* go first. Keep track of how many times you would have been right. Then, in two weeks, take the plunge."

Carla looked relieved. Mrs. Mather was smiling. "And Carla, I'll try to remind you more often how well you are doing. You may not realize it, but your classmates recognize that you are a very good math student. In fact, I think some of them would feel a lot better if they knew you make an occasional mistake. It makes you more like the rest of them."

Carla grinned, and nodded her head. "I get what you mean, Mrs. Mather. Thanks."

Recognize the Strength

A child with such a courteous, humble spirit may be like a breath of fresh air. Carla lacks confidence to go first because of her need to be right. You can help your child turn apparent timidity into strength by encouraging her to "look before she leaps"—but to go ahead and *leap* if she's sure!

Focus on Accountability

Mrs. Mather took an insightful approach with Carla, praising her natural mathematical ability and coaching her toward becoming more confident. The idea of keeping a private running tally for two weeks acted as a confidence booster. The two-week limit also gave Carla a chance to be a spectator, with the goal of taking a more active role later on.

It's always scary for a child to be wrong—especially in front of peers. If you have a child who seems timid or shy, let him or her practice making presentations at home. Encourage a trial run by letting them verbalize thoughts, explain a math problem, practice a report, or solve a problem out loud. Although practice may not make perfect, it certainly is a great confidence booster!

~ 27 ~

He's Too Analytic to Read

Sara Nelson was very proud of her first-grade son, Nathan. His teacher had told her how bright and capable Nathan was and how quickly and eagerly he had learned to read. His teacher also mentioned how analytic Nathan appeared to be, how he seemed to stop and figure out the whys of almost everything.

Sara smiled to herself. That was Nathan, all right. From the very beginning he had moved just a little more slowly than the rest of the family. Although she had been worried at first that he was a "slow learner," she soon discovered that Nathan was simply more deliberate, refusing to move on to the next task until he fully understood and finished the first one.

It was almost time for the nightly bedtime story, and Sara had purchased a brand new book she thought Nathan would like. The words were simple enough so that he should be able to read the entire text. She peeked into his room and found him comfortably settled in his bed, waiting for her.

His eyes lit up when she gave him the new book.

"I want to read it myself!" he insisted.

His mom sat next to him as he began to read the story. He didn't even hesitate when he read about the goat whose owners accidentally left the gate open. The goat escaped and began to eat and destroy many things. When the children who owned the goat returned, they would be very sad.

Then, Nathan began to stumble over several words. His mom was surprised. He had just read these very same words at the beginning of the story. Now he seemed to stop at even the simplest word, and he even mixed up the words *goat* and *gate*. He seemed to be concentrating intensely, but his reading got worse. Sara felt concern. What had happened? He had been doing so well!

Suddenly, Nathan put the book down in frustration. "Mom," he said with disgust. "If that goat's owners had just used an automatic gate closer, the gate would never have come open and the goat would never have gotten out and none of this stuff would have *happened*."

Sara almost laughed aloud. "Nathan!" she exclaimed. "Is that what you've been thinking about while reading the story? Were you busy thinking about how to fix the problem?"

He nodded and she hugged him.

"Honey, you are very smart to have figured out what the owners should have done. Of course, if they *had* used an automatic gate closer, there wouldn't really be a story for us to read, would there?"

Nathan shook his head. "But it's kind of a dumb story," he protested. "They just weren't *thinking*."

His mom put the book on his shelf. "Well, you can be sure *I'll* be thinking—especially when I buy you a book that has a problem to solve!"

Nathan gave her a goodnight kiss. "Mommy, how about next time I choose the book?"

"Great idea, Nathan. As a matter of fact, you're full of great ideas!"

Recognize the Strength

A logical mind such as Nathan's is constantly working out solutions to problems, and is a marvelous asset in today's business world.

Focus on Accountability

Step-by-step, logical thinking may slow down the process of reading for some children. If the child is trying to solve the problems of the story while reading it, the resulting confusion can often be straightened out when the adult and the child discuss the story. Letting your child verbalize his or her thought processes gives you an opportunity to straighten out any misunderstandings, and may help your child read more fluently.

～ 28 ～

Stick with the Plan

"What's the plan, Mommy?" Five-year-old Kelli looked expectantly at her mother. Ruth Barnes felt frustrated.

"Kelli, sweetie, I'm not sure yet. I need to find out what we're doing after I pick you up from school today."

Kelli looked concerned. "But Mommy, today is Wednesday. We always go to SKIP club on Wednesday."

Ruth reached out and put her arm around the worried little girl.

"Kelli, it's *OK*. We probably *will* go to SKIP club. It's just that a few other things have come up and I have to figure out how to do them all."

Kelli was beginning to panic. "But will I still get to go to *school?*"

Ruth was beginning to lose patience. "Oh for heaven's sake, stop *worrying*. I'll make sure you get to school, and I'll pick you up, just like always."

"And *then* what?" asked Kelli. Before her exasperated mother could answer, Dad walked in. Kelli almost knocked him down with the force of her hug. Tears were threatening to spill over onto her cheeks.

"Daddy! I can't go to SKIP club! Mommy doesn't know the plan!"

Mr. Barnes grinned at his wife. He picked Kelli up and set her on his lap.

"Kelli, Mommy *does* usually have a plan—she just doesn't always know the exact time things are going to happen. You and I like to know exactly what we're going to do ahead of time, but Mommy kind of plans as she goes."

Kelli looked confused. "OK," her dad said, "let's talk about what we definitely know, and then we'll talk about what we *think* will happen, and then what *might* happen. All right?"

"All right!" Kelli snuggled close and watched her dad's face intently.

"Well, we *know* that this morning you will finish breakfast, brush your teeth, and go to school. We *think* that your teacher, Mrs. Miles will be there. She *might* be gone, and in that case you would have a very nice substitute teacher."

Kelli nodded, and Dad went on. "After school, we *know* that Mommy or Daddy will pick you up. We *think* you'll go to SKIP club, like always, but you *might* end up running some errands with Mommy." Kelli seemed to enjoy the *know, think, might* game.

"Then what, Daddy?"

"Well, then we *know* you'll come home and get ready for bed. We *think* you'll go to sleep right away, but you *might* have to get up before you fall asleep to get a drink of water. But wait! I thought we *knew* you'd finish breakfast. It's getting late, so you only *might* barely have time to eat that cereal!"

Kelli giggled and slipped off Daddy's lap and into her chair. As she began eating her cereal, Ruth came over and gave her husband a quick hug.

"Thanks, honey. I sometimes forget how important it is to her to have everything planned and predictable. You know me, I just like going with the flow."

Her husband nodded and smiled. "That's why you have *me*," he reminded her. "After all, one of us has to help our daughter with 'the plan'!"

Recognize the Strength

Kelli, and children like her, are logical, sequential thinkers, and having a plan for the day provides great security for them. If you, as a parent, are not so sequential in your thinking, you may never have appreciated those who are very focused on details. These kinds of learners can become great administrators, consultants, organizers, and planners because they scarcely ever leave anything unplanned or unexamined.

Focus on Accountability

Not everyone needs the security of a plan. For those children who do, it's comforting to have an adult lead them through the predictable parts of their day. Even if "the plan" appears sketchy and full of gaps from an adult perspective, the child still finds comfort in knowing that parts of the day are planned. Turning the planning into the "think, know, might" game was a wonderful gift from Dad to Kelli. Some children, like Kelli, are auditory and like to talk through the plan. Others may be visual and will need to see the plan written down. Instead of becoming frustrated with a child who needs so much detail to be comfortable, enjoy the thinking and planning they display. It is a skill that will help them greatly in life.

~ 29 ~

What If "Time Out" Doesn't Work?

It was going to be another one of those days. Paula Anderson sighed. How could one small toddler upset an entire household so quickly?

Tyler was barely three, but he seemed to have the physical strength of a child twice his size, and the lung capacity of an adult chimpanzee. From the moment he escaped from his bed at 5:00 A.M. to the time he had knocked over the gallon of milk at breakfast, Tyler had been going full speed ahead.

He is a very determined child, thought Paula. *Someday that will be a good thing. Won't it?*

Her mind was too tired to agree with her heart, and Tyler had disappeared from the kitchen. *Uh oh,* she thought, *I'd better find him fast.*

He was in the bathroom, filling the sink. He had turned the water on full blast and it was overflowing onto the floor.

"Tyler!" she screamed. "You *know* better than that! I *told* you to leave the faucet alone!"

Tyler giggled with delight and splashed his mother with one of his favorite bathtub toys in the too-full sink.

"That's it!" she yelled. "It's *time out* for you! Get to your room *now!*"

"*NO!*" he replied. "I don't want to!" She reached down and picked him up. He stiffened his body and began kicking and screaming. Paula struggled to keep her balance amidst his flailing arms and legs.

She literally dragged him to his room, not sure which of them was shouting the loudest. It took all her strength to push his rigid body inside the bedroom. She had barely closed the door when he began to pound angrily and scream, "No! I don't want to be in my room!"

She held the door knob firmly with both hands, while the whole door frame suffered the onslaught of his fists and feet.

How much longer can I hold this? she thought. *How can he be so strong?* Then something occurred to her.

Which one of us is really being punished? Suddenly she stepped away from the door. Instantly an angry, red-faced little boy tumbled out.

Paula said nothing. Tyler eyed her suspiciously, but when he only got a noncommittal stare in return, he decided to go for it. Racing back into the bathroom, he began to splash water wildly. This time, Paula scooped him up and held him in her arms.

"No," she said simply. Tyler began to squirm and fight to get away, but she strengthened her grasp.

"Tyler, no. I will not let you make a mess in the bathroom. If you want to play with your toys in the water, you can take another bath. Right now, you and Mommy are going to clean up this mess."

Tyler was so surprised by the sudden turn of events, he stopped resisting. Paula pulled down two large towels. "Do you want the blue towel or the green one?"

He hesitated before deciding to cooperate. "Blue," he said with a sulking voice.

Paula began mopping up the water, paying little attention to the boy standing in the doorway uncertainly, holding a dry towel. Finally he began to dab at a little water with his towel.

When they were done, she turned to him. "Tyler, are you feeling nice enough to act like a good boy now?"

Tyler nodded.

"Do you want to take a bath?"

He shook his head.

"I love you, Tyler" she said. "I don't want any more messes like this, OK?"

"OK," he said in a small voice.

She hugged him and they headed toward the playroom. One down, she thought. *I'll bet it's going to take me awhile to get the hang of this.*

As she watched Tyler head for the cat sleeping peacefully in the corner, she realized the next showdown could be just moments away.

Recognize the Strength

Underneath Tyler's strong will is strong resolve to press toward a goal. It is important for a parent to learn to recognize and direct this strength of will and energy toward worthy outcomes and meaningful projects.

Focus on Accountability

The most important way to reach this child is to provide lots of love and a choice. Try not to issue ultimatums. "You will do this..." or "you will not..." are guaranteed to back strong-willed kids into a corner, with no choice but to come out fighting. Because a strong-willed child feels trapped as soon as he hears an ultimatum, you will soon find yourself in a battle of wills with him.

Two goals are achieved by first explaining your expectations as Paula did with Tyler, and then providing a couple of choices for your child. One: it keeps your authority as the parent intact, even as you communicate to your child that you respect him or her and that you will allow some freedom of decision in the matter. Two: when the strong-willed child is given some choices, regardless of how small they may be, cooperation happens more easily because he or she feels a sense of some control in the final outcome. When this type of child has input into the solution, it usually creates a win-win for both the parent and the child.

~ 30 ~

Lose That Smart Mouth

It was becoming a familiar scenario. Robin Crandall was sitting in the principal's office again, surrounded by her parents and two of her teachers. They were directly facing a very unhappy school administrator.

Mr. Farris had been the principal only a short time at Adams Junior High School, but he'd already seen more of Robin than any other student. He leaned forward and began the conference.

"Mr. and Mrs. Crandall and Robin, I believe you know why we are all here. Robin, you have been talking back to your teachers again. You know we cannot allow a smart-mouthed response to adults in authority."

Robin shrugged. "So sue me. But you'll have to stand in line or take a number."

Mr. Farris' face flushed beet red. "That, young lady, is exactly what I mean. You seem to have a smart comeback for everything."

"At least I'm smart," replied Robin.

Mr. Crandall reached over and placed his hand on his daughter's arm.

"Robin, that's enough," he said quietly.

Robin frowned and leaned back in her chair. Mr. Farris looked sternly at her.

"Robin, this has gone too far. Your teachers have given you several chances to clean up your act, and things have just gotten worse. It seems you have no respect for authority."

Robin shrugged again. "I don't mind authority. But I've got a real problem with how my teachers *use* it. I just don't think they respect me. So I don't respect them, either."

"Young lady," began Mr. Farris, "you don't get a choice here of whether or not to respect your elders."

Robin nodded. "Yeah, well, maybe that's the problem."

Robin's dad spoke up.

"Robin, you are not helping the situation here. Mr. Farris, I'm truly sorry my daughter is having difficulty with her teachers. This is not the first time in her life that her smart mouth has gotten her in trouble."

Robin sat back in her seat, sulking. Mr. Crandall continued. "Robin *does* have a quick wit and a sharp mind. I think until she learns to use her resources wisely, she is destined to be in and out of trouble. I would sincerely like to work with you *and* Robin to find a solution."

Mrs. Lander, Robin's Language Arts teacher, spoke up.

"Mr. and Mrs. Crandall, Robin has a real gift for writing comedy. Unfortunately, we haven't had any assignments that *call* for that particular talent, so her sense of humor has not exactly been appreciated." She looked at Robin.

"Robin, I'd like to see what you could do with writing a comedy script. Maybe a sample dialog for a TV sitcom or a standup comedian. I'd be willing to substitute that for your current essay assignment."

Robin gave her a noncommittal look, but seemed to be thinking about the proposal.

Mr. Unger, Robin's math teacher, spoke next.

"Unfortunately, math doesn't often *have* a humorous side. Robin, I can't let you turn my math class into a verbal dueling match. But I'll grant you we could use lightening up once in awhile. Suppose you and I devise a mathematical code that you could use periodically when you just can't stand to be quiet another minute. You could flash me that code, and I could let you vent for a moment—provided you didn't use profanity and you weren't personally insulting to anyone in class, including me."

Robin looked doubtful. Mr. Farris looked at her.

"Robin, the bottom line is that you are running out of options. These two teachers are being more cooperative than most would be, and frankly, I think they are being very generous. You already have some serious detention time coming. The next step is suspension from school. Do you want to give these suggestions a try?"

Robin frowned. "I don't know why you all can't just lighten up."

Robin's mom spoke for the first time.

"Robin, it's a little hard for people to appreciate your sense of humor when it's directed *against* them. Maybe you just don't realize how many people are hurt when you throw your little verbal arrows. Believe me, I often wish I could have thought of comebacks as quickly as you do. I admire your ability to think on your feet. But you are letting one of your best assets become your greatest liability."

Mr. Farris stood to his feet. "OK, Robin. The choice is yours. If you want another chance to succeed, you can agree to try what we've talked about here. Otherwise, say the word and I'll write the suspension notice."

Robin gave her typical shrug, but she did look interested. "I'll give it a shot," she agreed.

Recognize the Strength

Robin thinks faster than the adults in her world. Working with a child like Robin, helping her choose her words more carefully, helping her come to grips with how her words negatively influence those around her, may help the quick wit to be displayed in a more appropriate manner.

Focus on Accountability

Sarcasm, combined with a quick wit, helps many people become great comedians and talk-show hosts. Comedians like Jay Leno and Rosie O'Donnell are great examples of adults who have perfected the use of wit and sarcasm and have combined it with a great sense of timing.

Unfortunately for most children, these traits are often construed as flippancy and disrespect. Robin Crandall has a bit of refining to do, but the raw talent is apparent. If her teacher can help direct her junior-high energy, and show her how to combine it with her writing talent and sense of humor, she has the potential to become a great communicator.

～ 31 ～

Stop Taking Things Apart

Diane Clark's mother was holding an alarm clock that appeared to be in several pieces.

"Diane!" she called.

"In a minute, Mom!" Fourteen-year-old Diane called cheerfully. Mrs. Clark walked into her daughter's cluttered room.

"Diane, what happened to my alarm clock?"

Diane looked up from her desk, where she had spread several pieces from her battery-operated pencil sharpener.

"Oh, sorry. I just wanted to find out how the snooze alarm worked. I was going to put it back together. I forgot."

Diane's mom dropped the pieces of the clock into the wastebasket.

"Diane, this has to stop. You're costing us too much money. Everything around here that has moving parts is subjected to your analysis. You're very good at taking things apart, but you don't seem very interested in putting them back together."

Diane looked guilty. "I know, Mom. I'm trying, really. It's just that I like figuring things out, but I get frustrated when I try to put them back together."

Mrs. Clark sat down on Diane's bed.

"Tell me, Diane, what is it about taking things apart that appeals to you? Do you want to learn to *fix* things?"

Diane thought for a moment. "No, honestly I don't like the fixing part, just the taking apart part."

Mrs. Clark nodded. "Well, if you only take things apart and don't put them back together, that's going to be pretty hard on our possessions. We're going to have to figure something out. Is it machinery you like, or just small appliances?"

Diane shrugged. "I don't know, Mom. I just like messing with things and seeing what's inside."

Mrs. Clark thought for a moment. "Diane, why don't we visit the community college? Let's just see if they have any non-credit classes that include taking apart or fixing small engines or appliances. You could find out just how much interest you have in learning to do something with this constant desire to get inside any object that has working parts."

Diane brightened. "OK. But if I don't like the class, can I do something else?"

Mrs. Clark shook her head. "Not if we pay for the class. You need to at least finish one class before going on to the next. Who knows? Maybe finishing the class will help you decide how to actually *finish* a fix-it project as well!"

Diane smiled. "Hey, Mom, is that a new watch you're wearing?"

Recognize the Strength

The constant curiosity and creative desire to explore the unseen world inside an object shows a great mind at work. Enjoy this spark of creative curiosity by stretching a child's natural abilities and by guiding his or her energy toward appliances or items you no longer need.

Focus on Accountability

If your child, like Diane Clark, has a burning desire to tinker, try having a drawer, basket, or bin with a collection of inexpensive or broken items available for tinkering. Take such children to garage sales, second-hand stores, or thrift shops, so they can buy some inexpensive, used items to take apart. Perhaps giving the child a small allowance to spend during these trips would help him or her to understand that the things he or she is taking apart cost money.

The child needs to understand that dismantling anything that sparks his or her curiosity needs first to be cleared with the owner of the item. There also needs to be an understanding that taking things apart is only half the challenge, putting it back together again is the other half.

Encourage these children's curiosity by finding classes in small appliance repair; or perhaps you could even find a mentor who would work one-on-one with your child. Whatever you do, foster creative curiosity rather than squelch it. You have the makings of an artist, architect, doctor, or inventor on your hands. Keep the spirit alive!

~ 32 ~

The Money's Burning a Hole in His Pocket

Ryan Haley had several weekend lawn mowing jobs in the neighborhood and earned about $35 each week. He considered himself to be pretty rich. Although the mowing tied up a large chunk of time on Saturday, he liked knowing he would have a bulge of cash in his wallet after the weekend.

As he left for Leslie Middle School on Monday morning, he grabbed a couple of bills and crammed them into his jeans pocket. He wasn't sure what he might need, but was sure the money would come in handy.

"Hey, Mike," Ryan said as they climbed on the bus together. "You did a great job pitching last night."

"Thanks. I had to ice my shoulder while I did my algebra problems."

"Are you all right?" a worried Ryan asked.

"Yeah, I think it will be OK by practice on Thursday."

As they stepped off the bus and headed to their lockers, Ryan suggested, "Hey, I'll get you some bubble gum at the school store. That will keep your mind off your shoulder."

Ryan pulled the bills out of his pocket, set one on the counter, grabbed enough gum and penny candy for both Mike and himself and shoved the change back in his pocket. They headed down the hall.

"Thanks, Ryan. You're a great friend," Mike said.

"It's nothing," Ryan told him as they parted ways. "See you fourth period."

At lunch he grabbed some extra milk and some beef jerky sticks to share with Josh.

"Hey, Ryan, got an extra twenty-five cents I can borrow?" Rob yelled.

"Sure." Ryan flipped the quarter through the air.

Josh looked at him and said, "You always have money in your pockets to give away. Lucky dude. Wish I did."

Ryan smiled in an embarrassed way. "I work hard for it and it's fun to spend."

He grabbed a couple of cans of root beer out of the pop machine by the gym. He and Mike were always thirsty after PE, and it was soothing to have something to drink on the hot bus ride home.

Tuesday, Ryan and Rob stopped by the music shop to pick up some grease for their horns. "Hey, Rob," Ryan whispered. "Here's the sheet music for *Phantom of the Opera*. Let's get it and we'll have something to practice besides our band music."

"Rats," Rob said, "I'm broke."

"That's OK," consoled Ryan. "It's only $4.95 for each book, I'll just get both of them. You can pay me back later."

Wednesday and Thursday were typical middle school days, a few bucks here, some loose change there. Friday meant a baseball game, popcorn, a round of red licorice ropes for his friends, and a stop at the ice cream shop on the way home. Ryan's stomach seemed to always be empty, and his wallet was getting that way fast.

Saturday morning at breakfast, Ryan announced, "Dad, I need $65 for youth retreat, and I need a new pair of tennis shoes because the soles on my old ones are falling apart."

Mr. Haley smiled and asked, "How much money have you saved from mowing to put toward camp? Remember our forty/sixty bargain—you pay forty percent and we pay sixty percent of your recreation budget. Have you saved your part?"

Ryan frowned. "Nope, I don't have anything. I'll make another $35 today so I'll have that much." *Ugh, but I won't have even one dollar to spend at school next week,* he thought. A whole week without splurging on himself or his friends was going to cramp his style.

Mr. Haley interrupted his son's thoughts. "Mom and I need some warning about upcoming expenses. If we need to contribute $45 toward your retreat expenses and pick up the expense of your tennis shoes, that's at least $100 out of our budget this week. You're telling me you spent *all* of your mowing money last week?"

"Dad, I just couldn't help it. I don't know where it all went. I didn't buy any big things. I just spent a little at the school store each day, and some on lunch stuff, and some on my friends, and I guess it's just gone," he admitted sheepishly.

Mr. Haley had a stern but loving look on his face. "Son, we're proud of you for your generosity toward others, but you have to budget for your own needs. Perhaps we need to set up some type of system so you can learn to budget ahead. What do you think?"

"Hmmm. Yeah, we'd probably better do that. But can we talk later? Right now I gotta run. I've got some mowing to do and some money to make."

"Sure, son, we can talk later."

Recognize the Strength

Generous children who put others before themselves will grow up to be helpful, caring adults—something this world desperately needs.

Focus on Accountability

The "money burns a hole in his pocket syndrome" seems to be a common thread found in most families. Helping children learn to budget money at a young age will help them manage larger quantities of money as they move into their adult years. Their training may mean some monitoring on the part of their parents. Setting up a system, whether it is recycling soup cans into banks, using envelopes as a place to stash cash, buying a box with multiple compartments for portioning out money, or finding some other method of categorizing their money is fairly simple. You can label the compartment, cans, or envelopes with titles like "saving," "spending," "church," "recreation," "birthday/Christmas," or whatever works for your child's age and family situation. When children earn money, helping them decide how much to put in each category and offering some guidelines about how, when, and where to spend the money will develop habits that will transfer into adulthood, and can help those children become careful financial managers.

～ 33 ～

Finish One Thing Before
You Start Another

Beth Karnes seemed to be a model child. At eight years of age, she loved life and people. She used perfect grammar and was more polite than most adults, saying "please" and "thank you" almost more than was necessary. Her appearance was like something out of a fashion magazine for kids, and her beautiful, wavy red hair complemented her ivory skin.

So how could this perfect kid be so frustrating? Mrs. Karnes confided in Beth's teacher, Mrs. Hawke. "I just don't know how to help Beth finish one task before she starts another. Even as a toddler, she would roam all over the house, playing with blocks for a few minutes, then move on to Play-Doh, then puzzles. I tried everything to get her to put one thing away before starting another, but I can't find the magic trick. Now it's starting to affect her school work."

Mrs. Hawke, a very creative teacher, nodded. "Yes, I, too, have noticed this trait in Beth. She's always very eager to start a new subject, but has trouble concentrating for a lengthy lesson. She wants to move on to the next subject before we even finish our papers. She loves the art projects and science experiments we do, but she rarely completes them."

Mrs. Karnes was beginning to feel despondent. If this trend was being confirmed in third grade, and Beth still had many years of school yet ahead of her, what could she do? How could she get her daughter to finish one project before starting another? Could she break this frustrating cycle of half-done projects lying around that were being buried by other almost-done-but-never-finished projects?

As the frustrating thoughts filled Mrs. Karnes' head, Mrs. Hawke cautiously spoke up. "Beth has some incredible talents. She is very

113

creative. Some of the stories she has written during our creative writing lessons have shown a depth of maturity and a flair for communicating the written word that most adults haven't mastered. Even as a third-grader, I believe her random thought process is a glimpse of a creative, free mind that has the potential to become a creator, an artist, a writer, a truly gifted adult."

"But," said Mrs. Karnes, "how can she ever be successful and accomplish great things if she can't even finish one project?" She felt hopeless, but continued to listen to Mrs. Hawke.

"Beth has many, many talents. She is bright and capable. Just because she isn't great at finishing projects doesn't mean she is a failure. She has a long, bright future ahead of her. We need to do what we can to help develop the skills she has. We have to hold her accountable for her work. I will do what I can with her work at school, and I'll try to communicate with you weekly about her progress. I'll let you figure out what to do on the home front. In the meantime, take heart. This is not an insurmountable problem. I'm sure we can work on this together. Beth has so much potential, I'm sure she will someday be the creative force for some great business."

"You're so encouraging, Mrs. Hawke. Thank you for being so positive. It has helped me put things in perspective with Beth. I look forward to your weekly notes." Mrs. Karnes left the school relieved, encouraged, and challenged.

Recognize the Strength

Children who are random thinkers are often random and scattered with their projects as well. These individuals usually have great creativity. Random thinkers see and think wondrous things that are missed by those who stay on the path or think in a straight line. They just view life from a wider, more varied perspective. This way of thinking can be a great gift to share with others.

Focus on Accountability

Many tasks in life need to be completed as well as started. Helping your child bring closure to projects, or finish assignments, will help him or her have a deeper sense of accomplishment. In order for it to happen, you may have to monitor your child's work and progress—checking in frequently about deadlines and due dates. Help these children as much as you can without doing the work for them. Remember, random thinkers are just wired differently than more sequential thinkers. It may ease some of your frustration and may help your child understand that closure is important to some people and some jobs, but the priorities and methods of getting there are bound to be different.

～ 34 ～

Talk, Talk, Talk

Dennis dialed the phone. "Hey, Jeff, it's me."

"Hi, Den. Whaddaya need?" Jeff asked.

"I was just wondering about something. In Social Studies today, Mr. Hodges was going on and on about the differences between American culture and Pacific Rim culture and I don't get it. What is culture anyway?" Dennis asked, half yawning.

"I think you were whispering to Melanie when Mr. Hodges was defining 'culture.' Anyway, it has to do with what defines you as belonging to a group of people." Jeff succinctly summarized the lesson.

"Oh—like skin color and the clothes we wear?" Dennis inquired.

"Yeah, that's part of it. I've made a great chart comparing the two. It's an easy way to see the differences. I'll show it to you in class tomorrow. Talk to you later."

Jeff is a life saver on this one, thought Dennis.

He didn't even hang up the phone. After pushing the hang-up button and getting the dial tone, he dialed Melanie's number.

"Hello," Melanie said.

"Hi, Babe. It's me. Just thought I'd check and see how you are feeling," Dennis yawned again.

"My throat still hurts. I think I'll stay home tomorrow. Would you take good notes in Social Studies class? I missed something today about culture and I wasn't following Mr. Hodges' comparisons very well. Guess I just wasn't feeling well," Melanie said with a thick sound to her voice.

"Yeah, me too. Jeff has some kind of chart he said will help. I'll get a copy for you. Take it easy and I'll call tomorrow." Dennis was just hanging up when his mom walked into the room.

"You've been on the phone quite awhile, Dennis," she suggested.

"Can you take a break so anyone trying to reach us can get through?"

"Sure, Mom." Dennis grabbed the TV remote and did some quick channel surfing while he walked to the kitchen to get a drink of water. A commercial he flipped past gave him a great idea. He quickly dialed Roger.

"Hey, Rog. I just got a great idea for our media project for Communication Class next week." Mrs. Johnson returned to the family room moments later, only to find Dennis talking on the phone *again*. She gave Dennis the thumbs down sign and frowned at him.

"OK. I gotta get off the phone. We can talk about it at lunch tomorrow...yeah...bye." Dennis carefully placed the phone on the receiver. "Sorry, Mom, I just had this great idea I had to run past Roger...it's for..."

Mrs. Johnson smiled and patted her son on the shoulder as he explained the last call. *He's been talking practically since the day he was born*, she mused, *I doubt he's going to change at age seventeen*.

Recognize the Strength

Dennis may be an auditory learner which means he just needs to talk in order to think. He will probably be a very expressive adult, in either oral or written form, and may choose a career such as teaching or sales and marketing where talking is important.

Focus on Accountability

Kids like Dennis who talk during class when they should be listening will undoubtedly pay the consequences via grades or social embarrassment. However, even the consequences may not change their behavior. These kids need teachers who will build talk-time into lessons. If you have a talkative child, he is probably the type of learner who needs to talk to process information. It is only as he talks that information sinks in and sticks. Talk through his school day with him. Ask specific questions about each subject. "What are you studying in science this week?" or "What story are you studying in English class?" These are the questions that will help your child cement his learning.

~ 35 ~

Stop Clinging to Me

Jason Little was wandering around the house, yelling "Mommy, where are you?" He had a frightened look on his face, and his eyes were ready to overflow with tears. "Mommy, where are you?" His voice got louder and sounded as if it were ready to crack. "Mom... meee, where are you?"

Rhonda Little emerged from behind the bathroom door. "Honey, I'm right here." As she saw Jason's face, she fell to her knees, hands dripping wet, and hugged him. "Jason, honey, what's wrong? Mommy is right here. Tell me. What's wrong?"

"Nuffing is wrong. I couldn't see you. What you doing?" Jason began to relax and Rhonda loosened her hug.

"I'm just scouring the bathtub. I'm going to be right here working," she said, wiping the sweat off her brow.

"I bring my fings right here. I be here with you," he said running to get his action figures and some trucks.

Rhonda sighed. How could she clean the bathroom with a three year old and his toys under her feet? Not that this was a new problem. She was used to Jason wanting to be close to her all the time. Nearly every waking minute he was on her lap, hanging on her leg, holding her hand, or under her feet. It seemed like he was more an extension of her body than a little person of his own. In a way she enjoyed it. After all, eventually he would grow up, go off to school, and have his own group of friends, and she would no longer be an important part of his life. However, it was physically exhausting to have him touching her almost every moment of the day. She hardly had one free minute to herself to get dressed and put her makeup on in the morning. Even when her husband came home from work at night, she got very little reprieve. Jason loved Daddy, but didn't cling to him the way he did to her.

Her thoughts were interrupted again. Jason was tugging on her sweat pants. "Mommy, can you hold me and read me a story? Please Mommy, can you?"

"I'd love to, honey. You go pick out a book while I rinse the cleanser out of the tub. Let's turn this timer on for *two* minutes. You play while it ticks, and when it rings, I'll come read you stories, OK?"

Jason brightened, intrigued by the timer. "OK!"

Rhonda started the timer and quickly retraced her steps to the bathroom. *Only two minutes this time,* she thought, *but next time I'll make it three!*

When the timer rang, Jason rushed to the bookshelf in his bedroom to make his selection for story time. He pulled four of his favorite, well-worn books off the shelf. As he lugged them down the hall, he called, "I'm ready, Mommy. I'm ready for you to read."

Rhonda wiped her forehead with the back of her hand and then wiped her hands on the towel. She was ready to sit down for a break anyway. "I love you, honey," she said as she gratefully sank down into the softness of the sofa.

"I wuv you too, Mommy."

Recognize the Strength

It is exhausting to have such a demanding child, but the bonding that can occur between parent and child during these early years will have a lasting impact on your life-long relationship. When he is older Jason will probably be a devoted, loving parent to his own children, and very thoughtful and kind to his own parents.

Focus on Accountability

Jason seems to need a lot of attention, physically, emotionally, and psychologically. Using the timer may be a good method for slowly weaning Jason away from Mommy, so that he won't be traumatized in kindergarten and first grade when he has to be separated. If you are a parent facing this situation, try visiting a friend who has a child the same age so they can play together for a few minutes at a time. Enroll him or her in community-sponsored recreation classes or toddler-preschool classes that last at least one or two hours. Gymnastics, ballet lessons, tumbling, library story hour—anything that involves a small group of children whose attention is focused on a specific goal—will also help your child begin to center on people or places outside the immediate family and, particularly, Mom.

～ 36 ～

Video Game Wizard

"Bam! Bam! Bam! Rat-a-tat-tat!"

Ethan Rogers was lying nearly flat on his back in his bean bag chair, his head tilted up just enough to see the monitor, the joy stick in his hands and the remote by his side. "I gotcha now!" he yelled at the screen.

Little robots were hopping around, lights and flashes were popping everywhere. Then a big explosion lit up the screen. "YES! I WON! One hundred two million, seven hundred forty thousand, six hundred twenty-two points! My best score ever!"

Mrs. Rogers slowly entered the war zone consisting of the family room floor, Ethan and his chair, and all the paraphernalia that goes with a top-of-the-line home video game system. The shelf below the monitor was crammed with every type of video game you could imagine, and then some.

"Ethan," she calmly interrupted. "It's time for dinner. We'd like you to wash your hands and come to the dining room now."

"OK, but I just started this game, I'll be there in a minute," he said, his voice trailing off as his concentration deepened.

Mrs. Rogers sighed and returned to the kitchen. She knew the routine. The family would say grace, serve the food, and eat calmly over conversations about work and school. Ethan would arrive just as dishes were being cleared. His food would be cold, but even that wouldn't faze him. He would gulp down whatever was left and return to the video screen for several more hours of rabid attention to the seventeen-inch screen with its constant barrage of beeps, buzzes, flashes of color, and explosions. Cannons booming, war noises, and constant sounds of destruction filled the family room hour after hour. It happened again this night, just as she had predicted.

Mr. and Mrs. Rogers love their son, and have tried every way they know to get him interested in other forms of entertainment and exercise. But his driving passion at the moment is the constant noise of the battlefield screen and the ensuing flow of points to the scoreboard.

Ethan is an intelligent fifteen year old, who has never had to work very hard for grades. He has been reading well beyond his grade level since third grade, and considers school to be a boring prison sentence he must endure until he can graduate and flee to the real world. His social skills aren't the greatest, but he doesn't care. His video system is his best friend, and they understand each other quite well.

"Ethan," Mr. Rogers said gently as the lights and bells of the scoreboard started sounding.

"YES!" Ethan screamed, jerking his fist to his chest. "Oh, sorry, Dad, I didn't see you. Whatcha need?"

"Did you win again?" Mr. Rogers asked his son, already knowing the answer.

"Yeah! I just love this new game."

"Let's talk, son."

Ethan turned off his game and repositioned himself in the bean bag. "About what?" he asked casually.

"Your mother and I are concerned about the quantity of time you are spending in front of this machine. We didn't realize when we purchased it that you would become so addicted to it," Mr. Rogers explained cautiously.

"Dad, you make it sound like I'm doing drugs or something gross," Ethan complained with a grimace.

"Think about it for a minute. What does the word 'addiction' mean?" Mr. Rogers questioned.

Ethan frowned. "It's like when you're hooked or something. Like taking drugs and you can't stop."

Mr. Rogers nodded. "But it's not just drugs you can be addicted to, Ethan. I think you and I both know you're addicted to these video games."

Ethan shrugged, but he didn't argue. His finger was itching to get back to the game; he just wished his dad would hurry up with the lecture and move on.

"I've thought about just taking the whole system away," admitted his dad. Ethan looked startled and Dad quickly continued. "Then I realized that you're a young man, and we need to work this out differently than when you were younger. We love you and we want you to be happy, but we cannot live with your constant preoccupation with video games. You're still part of the family, and I want you to help us figure out how to solve this problem."

Ethan shifted restlessly in his seat. "Well, I guess I *could* cut back," he said slowly. "Like maybe not play during meals and family times."

Mr. Rogers nodded in agreement. "Ethan, I apologize for letting things get this far out of hand. Your mother and I should have stepped in sooner, and we feel bad that the situation has gone this far. We're willing to work with you to restore some kind of normal family life. We want you to know that we *are* committed to doing it, and it will be much easier if you help us. Can we count on you?"

Ethan stood to his feet and handed his father the joy stick. "Can I come back in an hour?" he asked.

Mr. Rogers gave him a quick pat on the shoulder. "Deal," he said. As Ethan left the room, Mr. Rogers felt that a small step had just been taken on a very long journey.

Recognize the Strength

Ethan may truly enjoy all the visual stimulation, as well as the opportunities for logic and problem-solving the games afford him. He is also very intelligent and the games may be stimulating his well-developed intellect, perhaps filling the void he feels because his classes aren't providing enough challenge.

Focus on Accountability

Mr. and Mrs. Rogers provided an entertaining and stimulating way for Ethan to occupy himself. Seeing how much their son enjoyed the games was probably gratifying on one hand and disturbing on the other. The Rogers may not have anticipated the social isolation that resulted for their son. If you have a child who is addicted to video games, setting limits on how much time he or she can spend playing games is important. So is including some educationally sound programming in addition to the games. When bright children like Ethan are under-challenged at school, they will turn to something stimulating elsewhere in their lives. It's a short step for them, then, to develop an addiction or dependence on this stimulation. Look for community college or community education classes that teach computer programming skills. Good programmers are going to be in demand in the business world from now on. If children like Ethan can play well, they can certainly learn related skills that could lead to some exciting career or business options as they approach adulthood.

～ 37 ～

You Aren't Wearing That, Are You?

"Have you seen what our son is wearing today?" Tom Harris kissed his wife Susan as he walked through the door.

"Oh no," she replied. "You *saw* him already?" She had fought quite a battle with Lonnie this morning before school. He had always been such a traditional, obedient boy. Suddenly, at fourteen, she barely recognized him. He had insisted on growing his hair long, and one day he had let his friends talk him into dyeing part of it green. Susan and Tom had agreed to try not to make too big a deal over his stab at independence, but Susan was struggling.

This morning when he had come downstairs, she just couldn't help herself. He had been wearing the newest fad—loose pants that rode at least halfway down his hips and bunched up for several inches above his feet. But the worst of it was a new accessory he was sporting in his left ear.

"An *earring?*" Susan was practically screaming at him. Lonnie seemed surprised at the force of her protest.

"What's the big deal, Mom?"

Susan tried to stay calm, but she wasn't very successful. "Lonnie, what in the world were you *thinking?* Why didn't you at least talk this over with us before you did it? What will your *father* say?"

Lonnie shrugged. "It's just what kids do now, Mom. I don't know why you're so upset."

"Since when do you do things just because others do them? Lonnie, you have always been such a *good* boy!" she exclaimed. She instantly wished she could take the words back when she saw the hurt look cross his face.

"Mom, I'm not a *bad* boy now. I think you take things way too seriously."

Susan didn't trust herself to continue the discussion and quickly sent him off to school without further comment.

Now, talking to her husband about it, she felt guilty about confronting Lonnie.

Tom sat down at the kitchen table. "Susan, we need to decide what we're going to do about this whole wardrobe issue. It's just going to become more of a problem as Lonnie goes through junior and senior high school. He's struggling to become independent."

Susan nodded. "I just always thought our 'independent' young man would grow up wearing suits, ties, and wing-tip shoes."

Tom grinned. "I think maybe we have to realize that how our son dresses is not necessarily a reflection of who he really is. He's still a great kid, Susan."

She nodded. "You're right. I have to admit, I've kind of blown the clothes thing out of proportion. After all, he is *dressed* every morning, and his schoolwork doesn't seem to be suffering."

"Why don't we talk to him tonight at dinner?" Tom suggested. "Let's remind him how much confidence we have in his ability and apologize for making a big deal about the way he looks."

Susan sighed. "I'm going to have to 'remind' myself not to look at that dreadful earring!"

"Susan, if that's the worst thing we have to adjust to right now, we are indeed blessed."

After school that day, Lonnie burst through the door.

"Hi, Mom, Dad. What do you think of this tattoo?" As he thrust his arm toward his mother, she almost fainted.

Lonnie grinned and hugged her. "I'm just kidding—it's temporary."

His mom gave him a playful punch. "Don't *do* that to me!" she told him.

"I still haven't decided what the permanent one will look like," Lonnie added.

"Son," his dad said, "we need to talk to you right after dinner."

Recognize the Strength

Outward appearance is not always an indication of inward convictions as much as society tries to have us believe. Adolescent children are trying out ways to separate their identities from that of their parents. They're trying to establish independence. Recognize that your child is an individual, one who is approaching adulthood. Respect his or her choices, even if the choices are different than you had hoped they would be.

Focus on Accountability

Children are pressured from all sides during adolescence. Their bodies are changing both inside and out, and they often wonder who their real selves are. It's so important for parents and teens to have open and honest communication. It's also important to show respect for your children's choices. At the same time, while you do respect their choices, you may need to have a frank discussion of bottom-line accountability issues and let them know what you can and cannot live with. Include a wide variety of topics in your discussion so that they don't feel you are zeroing in on only one issue. Ask them to tell you what *they* can and cannot live with.

If you each try to compromise a little to reach common ground, you will gain in mutual respect. Remember—choose your battles carefully. Is this issue life-threatening? Will it make any difference in two to five years? Will it bring life-long damage and regrets, or is this something that will blow over in a few weeks or months? Your reaction can really make a difference!

～ 38 ～

He's Never Ready for Bed!

"Michael! It's bedtime!" Rita Sherman knew she would have to give several more warnings before seven-year-old Michael finally started his bedtime routine. She wished she knew what else to try to get Mike into bed at his real bedtime. She'd argued, cajoled, bribed, threatened, and had finally given up. She was tired of the battle and had run out of options. Tonight she just wanted to get bedtime over with and sit down for a quiet cup of coffee with her next door neighbor, Virginia.

Virginia and her husband had moved in a few weeks ago, and it hadn't taken long for Rita and Ginny to become fast friends. As a single mom, Rita was grateful for another mom to talk to and lean on for a little moral support. Virginia's children were grown and had gone to college, so Rita felt confident in her maternal advice.

"Ginny, I swear it takes forever for that kid to finally get to bed." Rita plopped down in the living room chair. Virginia leaned forward.

"Rita, if you don't mind some advice, I think I might have a few ideas for Michael."

"I'm all ears, Ginny. Believe me, I'm ready for a second opinion."

"What's Mike doing right now?" asked Virginia.

Rita paused, listening for the sound of activity from upstairs.

"It sounds like he's still playing with the Legos," she said. "It kills him to leave a building project half finished."

Virginia nodded. "Sounds familiar. Jack was the same way. From the time he was a tiny kid, he simply had to finish one task before he could even think about going on to the next one. It was a real problem at bedtime until I realized that many times I let him start a project too close to bedtime. Since he wouldn't just stop and finish it the next day, we had many a battle over getting to bed on time."

Rita was thoughtful. "You know, Mike *is* a pretty thorough kid. He moves very slowly—just about drives me crazy! Since I can do so many things at once, I don't even think about how important it is to him to have a sense of closure."

Virginia smiled. "That will end up being a valuable trait if he uses it well. But at his age, he needs you to help him pace himself. He'll meet deadlines a lot better if he gets a sense of how much time it's going to take to complete each project. I'd say set the time for going to bed and help him work backwards to figure out what time it needs to be when he starts his last project of the night."

Rita stood to her feet. "You know, it's worth a try. It makes a lot of sense. Guess I'll go up and talk to Mike about it. That is, if he can tear himself away from his Lego project."

"Give him time," Virginia reminded her.

"I will. Thanks, Ginny."

Recognize the Strength

A child who becomes so engrossed in his play that he hardly notices the passage of time is very likely to be an adult who has great powers of concentration. The ability to concentrate no matter what is happening around you can be a wonderful gift.

Focus on Accountability

Ask the child how much time he or she wants to play with this toy. Then, working together, set a time schedule for bedtime. Include play time and all the nightly routines like taking a bath, putting on pajamas, brushing teeth, bedtime stories. Some children may enjoy having the schedule written out or printed out on the computer. If such children have a digital clock in their rooms or play areas, they can match the actual time to the bedtime schedule chart and begin making decisions about how to use the time wisely.

~ 39 ~

She Won't Do Her Homework

"Lisa Chambers, have you done your homework?" There was an inaudible mumble from the other side of the bedroom door, and although Lisa's mom knew what that meant, she opened the door and asked again anyway.

"Lisa, does that mean you *have*, or you *haven't*?" Her seventh-grade daughter was sitting at her new student desk, head in her hands.

"I'm through."

Mom eyed her suspiciously. "You may be *through*," she said, "but have you *done* anything?"

Lisa groaned. "Oh, Mom, I just can't *do* it!" She got up and plopped down on her bed.

Mrs. Chambers sat down in the chair vacated by her daughter and leaned forward. "OK, Lisa, we've got to *solve* this. Your grades are really slipping, mostly because you don't do the assigned homework. We bought you a new desk and lamp, got you the notebooks you wanted, and we promised you a $100 shopping spree at the mall if you got more than one *A* this next semester. But so far, nothing has worked. What next?"

Lisa shrugged. "I don't know, Mom. I just can't *concentrate*."

"OK. I accept that. But let's figure out *why*. You're comfortable on the bed right now. Do you think you might be able to work on your homework there better than at your desk?"

Lisa looked at her mom, amazed. "I thought you *wanted* me to use my desk."

Her mom shook her head. "Not if it doesn't work for you. Right now I'm more concerned with your getting the work *done* than with where and when you do it. What else do you think would help you concentrate?"

Lisa thought for a moment. "You wouldn't like it," she said, "but it's too quiet in here. I wish I could have my CD player on while I work."

Mrs. Chambers winced. *Surely the music would just be distracting,* she thought. But she nodded her head.

"Lisa, I'm willing to let you try, if you promise you'll work while you listen. Anything else?"

Lisa looked pleased. She was on a roll now—might as well go for it.

"I need something to eat or drink," she said. "My stomach growls, and it's hard to think when I'm hungry."

Her mom started to object. *Why can't she just eat before she starts her homework?* she thought. *Or reward herself by eating after she's done?* But again, she nodded in agreement.

"OK. It's certainly not what would work for *me*, but I'll give you a chance to prove it will work for *you*."

Lisa sat up eagerly.

"Do I still get the shopping spree if my grades go up?" she asked.

"Absolutely," Mom said and held out her hand for a handshake. "You've got a deal."

As she left Lisa's bedroom, Mom wasn't sure *which* one of them was most surprised by the conversation they had just completed. *I think maybe I just did some very important homework myself,* she thought.

Recognize the Strength

The desire to find the right environment for work is a benefit to both Lisa and her mom. Some children need noise, bright light, food, or a combination of these things to be able to concentrate. For some children, sitting on the floor or a bed or sprawled out in a big chair works better for study than sitting at a desk. Each of us has different preferences when we are concentrating on learning. Remember, chances are good that your children won't need the same environment you do to learn.

Focus on Accountability

The bottom line for both parent and child is that the homework is completed. The road to success is very different for Lisa than it would be for Mrs. Chambers. If you have a child like Lisa, you may need to re-evaluate how he or she accomplishes the homework. If location, food, music, or time of day have a heavy influence on how much or how long the child can concentrate, then try some alternatives to the way the child is studying now. If what you are trying to accomplish is an increase in learning and understanding during homework time, try as many alternatives as possible when arranging the physical setting. Keep the lines of communication open so you can continually evaluate all the options you try as you seek the best environment for learning.

～ 40 ～

But I Hate to Read

"I can't believe Mrs. Russell is making us read fifty-six pages by Friday! We're only in the seventh grade. She shouldn't make us read so much!" Cheryl Miller plopped into a chair in the living room and threw her books on the floor.

Her dad looked up from the newspaper and frowned.

"I don't think fifty-six pages is so much," he observed.

"Dad, I *hate* to read! It takes way too long, and I don't even know the big words!"

Mr. Miller put his paper down and looked carefully at Cheryl. He had thought reading would get easier for her as she got older. As a child she had loved having books read to her, but she had always avoided reading books herself. Her teachers had told him that Cheryl was bright and had a lot of potential. They hadn't seemed to think that her reluctance to read was that big a deal. But now she was thirteen, and hopefully headed toward college. Shouldn't she be reading more by now?

"Cheryl," he said, "why do you think reading is so hard for you?"

She looked at him impatiently. "Dad, I *told* you. It takes me a long time, and I don't understand what I'm reading. I don't know what the big deal is about reading anyway. Almost everything I like is turned into a movie anyway."

Her dad frowned. "Now *wait* a minute. Do you plan to get a job someday? Do you want to make your own money?"

Cheryl nodded. "Well, yeah—sure I do."

Her dad continued. "How many jobs let you just watch *movies* instead of reading?"

Cheryl shrugged. "I'll think of something," she said weakly.

Mr. Miller sat up straight in his chair, leaned toward her, and in

133

loving earnestness asked, "Cheryl, do you *want* to read better?"

She thought for a moment. What was she getting herself into?

"Sure I do. Who wouldn't? But I hate to read *boring* stuff."

"No one likes to read boring stuff," he answered. "But what if we started helping you practice reading books you really like?"

"I don't *know* any books I like," Cheryl admitted. "I just like to *talk* to people and *do* things, not sit down and read."

"Well, you'd make yourself a lot more interesting person if you read a lot of books," her dad replied. "Why don't we try to find a book that appeals to you as much as talking to your friends does."

A few minutes later they were standing in the youth section of a large bookstore. Cheryl seemed a bit overwhelmed by all the volumes on the shelves. Her dad sensed her confusion.

"Do you want to read a story, or would you rather read about how to do something?" he asked.

Cheryl answered quickly. "I'd rather have a story."

Mr. Miller guided her to the fiction section. "Just let your instincts draw you to a book. Don't worry about how many words or how difficult it looks to read. If it appeals to you, let's take a look."

Cheryl spent a few minutes browsing, and kept coming back to the same book.

"I like this one," she said. "But I can already tell you I can't read it."

Her dad waved aside her objection. "As a matter of fact, Cheryl, you don't *have* to read it—well, not by yourself, anyway."

Cheryl was puzzled. Dad took a package off the shelf.

"Here," he said, handing it to her. "It's the book read on tape. You can listen and follow along in the actual book. The person reading it will know all the words. I think you'll find it not only interesting, but I think it will help you learn the difficult words and understand the meaning of the story. What do you think?"

Cheryl nodded. "I guess I could try it," she agreed. "I think my friends would like this book, too. Maybe after I read it, I could let them borrow it."

As they waited to pay for the book, Mr. Miller stole a glance at his daughter. She was leafing through the book, looking genuinely interested in finding out what was in it.

I wish I had started this a few years ago, he thought.

Recognize the Strength

Cheryl is a strong auditory learner, which means she learns better by hearing and talking than by reading or watching. She has become very discouraged, since much of school work depends on visual learning. But there is a spark of desire for self-improvement in her, and her wise father has tapped it. He is working with Cheryl's desire to be a more interesting person, improve her reading skills, and be able to talk with her friends about current books and ideas.

Focus on Accountability

Literacy is highly valued in our society and is a stepping stone to successful education and career choices. It is important for parents and teachers to promote reading at every age. If you have a child like Cheryl, who would rather talk than read, or who is frustrated because of poor reading skills, be patient and persistent. Modeling good reading can occur in a variety of ways. Reading to your children daily is the number one way to teach them to read. Providing books on tape is another, and these are available at almost any reading level from preschool through adult.

～ 41 ～

Don't Take Things So Literally

Eleven-year-old Christina Barnes was reading a book about learning styles. Suddenly she stopped and asked her dad a question.

"Dad, what does it mean to be able to 'read between the lines'? There's nothing between the lines to *read!*"

Don Barnes chuckled. It was so like Christina to see only the obvious. "Well, Christina, it's being able to understand more than what is actually stated. To read between the lines, you have to know what something *means*, not just what it *says*."

She still looked confused. He tried again.

"Remember when you and I were at the grocery store the other day and we walked out the doors? You looked down and saw a warning painted on top of the curb that said *Caution: Step Down*. I thought the warning was a good idea to prevent falls, until you pointed out that it didn't make sense. You said if you weren't looking down already, you wouldn't see the warning, and if you *were* looking down you wouldn't *need* it in the first place. You just looked at what was very obvious, while I *read between the lines* and assumed the warning made sense."

Christina was nodding. "I *think* I get it. It's like when Mom and I were at the medical center and we went into the bathroom. When I was inside the little stall, I saw a sign that said *Please wash your hands before leaving this area*. I asked Mom how could I wash my hands in there when there was only a toilet. She said the sign meant the *whole* bathroom. But I still want to know why they put it *inside* the stall?"

Her dad laughed. "Yes, Christina, that's a great example of looking at the obvious instead of reading between the lines and assuming what someone meant."

Christina frowned. "Sometimes that makes me look *dumb*, doesn't it?"

Her dad shook his head. "No, Christina, you mustn't think that. You have a gift for looking at the here and now and dealing with the facts. That's a very good thing. But you just may want to practice looking *beyond* the obvious once in awhile."

Christina thought for a moment. "I don't think I know how to do that unless you help me," she said truthfully.

Her dad smiled and put his arm around her. "You know, I think I could use your help in reminding me to rely more on the facts and not assuming I know more than I do. I shouldn't look beyond my own nose so often."

Christina gave him a puzzled look.

"What does *that* mean?" she asked.

"Uh oh," he replied. "I'm going to have to start thinking about how to explain these things!"

Recognize the Strength

When a person processes information mainly by using their five senses, they interpret their world in a very literal fashion. It is what it is, and they assume no more. A child like Christina, who learns very concretely, will make decisions and judgments based on reality and the obvious.

Focus on Accountability

When an individual naturally focuses on the obvious and misses the hidden "between the lines" messages, he or she may need some guidance in the interpretation of hidden meanings. Using real-life stories to illustrate hidden meaning may be helpful. Giving one- or two-word clues may also lead the child's thinking toward the unstated. With maturity, children like Christina will be able to attempt more abstract thinking, even though it may never come easily and naturally to their way of thinking.

～ 42 ～

Guys Have Feelings, Too

They sat around the conference table, each one a little nervous about the direction this discussion was going to take.

Mr. Finch, the principal, nearing retirement, had a soft-spoken voice and a very calm spirit. Mr. Pierce and Mr. Carey were the physical education teachers at Cottonwood Junior High, and they had very high expectations regarding the performance of their athletes. Mark Miller and his dad were sitting across from the teachers, hoping this situation could be worked out.

"Gentlemen," Mr. Finch started the conference. "We're here today to try to come to some agreement about whether Mark will be allowed to return to the track squad and compete in the javelin throw at Saturday's regional meet."

Mark twiddled his thumbs under the table. He had said some pretty rash things to his coaches. No profanity or anything, but they had suspended him from competition until the issue was resolved. He knew he had probably been wrong, but at the time he had been reacting emotionally. He had not thought about the impact of his words.

Mr. Finch continued. "Mark, if I understand correctly, you made some derogatory statements toward your coaches last week. Is that true?"

"Yes, sir," said Mark, his voice a little shaky.

He turned and addressed the coaches. "Gentlemen, you've shared with me the details of the discussion, but would you mind recapping the events, so Mark and his dad and I can hear them again?"

Both coaches nodded. Mr. Pierce spoke first. "We had been running the boys, trying to build up their stamina and endurance. It was a training drill we had been doing all season. We had an understanding with the team that the track guys would run twenty laps around the track, thirty if everyone was not giving 100 percent toward the practice."

Mr. Finch turned back toward Mark. "Is this your understanding?"

"Yes, sir, but may I explain something else?"

"By all means," said the principal.

"All the guys knew about the ten extra laps if we didn't work hard. The problem was, we all felt like we were giving 100 percent and we'd done our regular practice and we'd run the standard twenty laps. It was eighty-three degrees and the drinking faucet out on the track was broken. We were begging for water and the coaches decided they had heard enough whining so they assigned us fifteen more laps on top of the twenty we'd already done. We were already dead. So I just got upset and told them we were people, not machines, and they were killing us. I probably didn't use a very nice voice, like not very respectful, when I was telling them." Mark let his voice trail off, and he could feel the emotion well up inside him again.

Hid dad leaned over and touched his hands. He whispered, "It's okay, son, but slow down. We're just getting the facts on the table."

"Mr. Pierce... Mr. Carey... is Mark recounting the incident correctly?" the principal inquired.

Mr. Carey spoke up this time. "We were laughing and teasing the guys. We hadn't really 'assigned' the fifteen laps; we had only said we might."

"No you didn't—well, yes—you did," Mark was flustered. "Wait. Let me explain. You were laughing, but you were laughing *at* us. We were serious. We were hot and tired. We were not laughing. Even though we're tough guys, we still have *feelings,* and we didn't like being laughed *at.* If you had been laughing *with* us, I wouldn't be sitting here right now." There, he'd said it. Guys have feelings, too. Just then, his dad leaned over and whispered again.

"Nicely said, son. Just let Mr. Finch handle this now," was his advice.

After a few more comments by the administrator, Mr. Finch turned to Mark. "Mark, I admire your position, although I want you to know that your original comments to the coaches were inappropriate," he admonished.

"Sorry, sir. I'll try not to let it happen again." Mark looked at his feet.

"Mr. Miller, we'd like it very much if Mark would return to practice to prepare for Saturday's meet," Mr. Carey said.

Mark's eyes lit up as his dad stood up and shook hands with Mr. Finch.

Mark stood up and reached out to shake hands as well. "I'll give it all I've got," he said, with a boyish grin.

"I trust you've learned an important lesson through this," Mr. Finch said with a knowing look.

The handshakes continued, with parting words of thanks. As they left the conference room, Mr. Finch gave Mark a quick thumbs-up and said, "We'll get that drinking fountain fixed this afternoon."

Mark grinned. "I had a feeling you would!"

Recognize the Strength

Mark was able to verbalize, even in the heat of battle, the need to be recognized and understood. Children who are bold enough and strong enough to speak for a group and confront the improper behavior of others, will be valued as friends and colleagues with character and integrity.

Focus on Accountability

Speaking disrespectfully to an adult in authority is unacceptable behavior. Mark needed to be confronted regarding this type of behavior toward his coaches. It was beneficial for all parties to sit at the table to hear both sides of the story and clear up the misunderstanding. Modeling this type of conflict resolution will help young adults who get into similar situations learn to work through disagreements in ways that keep respect intact for all parties involved.

～ 43 ～

Where Do I Start?

Mr. Root was explaining a new assignment to his sixth-graders. "This is a chance for you to be very creative. You need to think back over all of the geography topics we have studied—population, climate, topography, natural resources. You'll be designing your own island continent. It can be any shape you desire and located at any latitude and longitude coordinates where water is located. This assignment sheet has all the details."

Mr. Root continued explaining as he passed packets of information down each row of students. Hands started shooting up as the students minds raced over the possibilities.

"Mr. Root, can mine be the shape of a cat?" Sara blurted out.

"Mr. Root, can mine be a ski resort?" Ben asked, his knees bouncing back and forth as if he were already attacking a downhill run.

"Mr. Root, I want to have tropical beaches and surfing. Can mine just be Hawaii, and then I'll be done?" Shawn inquired.

"Nice try, Shawn, but no. Class, I think your imaginations have already kicked into gear. Remember, as long as you include all the items listed on page one of the assignment sheet, and you've stayed within the guidelines, you can be as creative as you wish," Mr. Root explained.

As he looked around the room, heads were already bent over and the students' pencils and erasers were in full use. Except for Cathy. Cathy was an excellent student. The quality of her work was always outstanding and she always included every detail a teacher asked for in perfect order. Often she included components that weren't assigned, because she deemed them necessary.

"Mr. Root, this is too big a project. How will we ever have time to get it finished by next Wednesday? There's just too much to think

141

about. I don't even know where to start," Cathy moaned.

"Cathy, why don't you start like most of your classmates, by sketching the shape of the island you want, making sure it has a peninsula, a bay, one major river, and all the rest of the items on this list," he said, pointing to page one of the assignment sheet.

"But I don't even know what type of climate I want on my island, and how can I make landforms if I don't know the coordinates where the island will be located?" Cathy complained with a very disgruntled look on her face.

"Cathy, I know you're good at analyzing the facts and paying attention to detail. Your project will be great when it's completed. Would it be helpful to just look at the globe for a few minutes while you let your mind wander over some possibilities?" Mr. Root smiled at her. "You try that while I answer a few other questions and then I'll get back with you."

Cathy wandered over to the counter and gently spun the globe around. *Mr. Root always had such patient, gentle words of encouragement,* she thought. *And he always gives me a suggestion for a place to start. I wish some of my other teachers would help me the way he does.*

Cathy decided, after spinning the globe slowly, that near Jamaica would be a great location based on prevailing trade winds and mild seasonal changes, as well as its proximity to the United States.

She returned to her desk and grabbed her pencil, knowing she would be spending many, many hours the next week making everything perfect.

Recognize the Strength

Being a perfectionist means a child like Cathy can focus on every detail and do a superb job of orchestrating an entire project to meet or exceed expectations. Cathy will be able to use this talent in the adult world of corporate management. These are the type of skills sought after in executive administrators or office managers. Keeping many people and many details organized and flowing smoothly is a valuable asset.

Focus on Accountability

Cathy and children like her enjoy having detailed projects to work on. However, finding the perfect starting point may be a frustration for them. Suggesting, as Mr. Root did, some possible starting places, and then occasionally checking on the progress these students are making, may help get them going. As these children grow and mature, it will become easier for them to identify their own starting place and monitor their own progress.

~ 44 ~

Is She Just Insecure?

Heather Lawson was a beautiful little girl. At nine years of age, she already possessed a great deal of poise, and her physical features were soft and graceful. But Heather's mother was concerned.

Sitting down together for an after school snack, Mrs. Lawson asked her, "Heather, why are you sad today? Something seems to be wrong."

Heather looked at her mother. "Mom, Mrs. Blackburn didn't say anything about my homework today. I worked really hard to get it all done, and she didn't say anything."

"Did you get credit for doing it?" her mother asked. "Did Mrs. Blackburn record the grade?"

Heather nodded. "But she didn't *say* anything," she insisted. "I don't think she likes me anymore."

Mrs. Lawson sighed. *Here we go again*, she thought. *Why is Heather so insecure?*

"Heather, of course she still likes you. She just doesn't *say* it all the time."

"*Nobody* says it all the time," Heather commented. Mrs. Lawson looked surprised.

"Do you feel like *we* don't like you?" she asked.

Heather frowned. "Well, it's not that I think you *don't* like me. It's just that you don't say you *do*."

Her mother reached over and hugged her. "Oh, Heather, your father and I *love* you, and we think you're wonderful. We just don't say it all the time." She paused. "Do you want us to remind you more often?"

Heather's eyes brightened. Then she shrugged. "Well, you don't have to if you don't *want* to."

Mrs. Lawson laughed. "Heather, don't be ridiculous! You're the light of my life!" She hugged her daughter again. "Hey, I've got an idea."

"What?"

"Heather, I'm afraid I just forget to tell you as frequently as I need to what a good job you're doing—or how nice you look. I'm trying to think of a way to remind myself."

"I know what to do!" said Heather excitedly. "How about if I remind you every day what I like about *you*? Then you might remember to tell *me* if I'm doing a good job or not."

Her mom nodded. "Great idea, Heather! But why don't you make it a practice to tell *everyone* you like and not just me? Every time I hear you tell someone something positive, I'll be reminded to tell *you* what I appreciate about you."

Heather smiled a radiant smile. "You really are a great mom!"

Mrs. Lawson grinned. "Heather, you just made it a lot easier! You are a wonderful daughter."

Recognize the Strength

Heather's yearning for positive affirmation is a need all people have. She just has a heightened desire for hearing it said out loud. As an adult, this need for affirmation and encouragement will help foster empathy and sensitivity toward the needs of others.

Focus on Accountability

Heather is constantly wanting verbal reassurances of others' love and acceptance, as well as positive feedback about her appearance, grades, work habits, and general importance. If you have a child who needs this kind of verbal reinforcement, consider something similar to Mrs. Lawson's approach. By encouraging children to praise others in a positive way, you are teaching them that the world is not centered around them, and that as they give compliments and positive words to others, they will eventually receive some in return. It's healthy for children to appreciate the strengths and value of others. It is the adult's job to help them learn how to give to others that which they appreciate receiving themselves.

～ 45 ～

Do You Know What I Like about You?

Donna Carter couldn't sleep. Her husband was snoring quietly, but she kept thinking about her two small children sleeping snugly across the hall. She was so blessed to have Jack and Kelsey! But she was also frustrated with the disparaging remarks that were now echoing in her head. She heard her own voice saying:

"Jack! Put the milk away, and don't forget to put the lid back on!"

"Kelsey! Don't lay that wet towel there—and put those clothes in the hamper!"

"Hey! Who left the dog's bed out in the rain?"

"Jack, this room is a *mess!* I'm going to have to give these toys away to someone else!"

"Kelsey, you're not getting any new clothes until you learn to take care of the ones you've got."

Donna frowned in the darkness. She tried to remember even one positive comment she had made during the day. Her frown deepened as the voices of her children crept back into her head:

"Jack, You're stupid and ugly. Get out of my room!" Kelsey screamed.

"Kelsey," Jack teased, "you're a baby, just like your dolls!"

"Annie, you're a bad dolly. You wet your pants," Kelsey said to her doll during a tea party.

"Little Jack Carter, sat in the corner, sucking his thumb. Na, na, na, na," Kelsey mimicked.

Donna sighed. She tried to remember even one positive comment she had heard either of her children make, but none came to mind. *I'm not a bad mother*, she told herself, *but I'm not being a very good role model when it comes to helping these kids encourage each other.* Sleep was delayed until she finally thought of a plan.

Early the next morning, five-year-old Kelsey crept into her parents' room and burrowed under the warm covers next to her mom. Donna roused herself and hugged her daughter.

"Hey, Kelsey," she said quietly. "Do you know what I like about you?"

Kelsey snuggled closer. "No," she whispered. "What?"

Donna smiled. "I like how you always seem to know when I need a hug. And you know what else?"

"What?"

"I really like it when you share your toys with your brother, and when you are very careful not to mess with his stuff. That's very thoughtful."

Kelsey looked up at her mom with a big smile. "Hey Mom, you know what?"

"What?"

"I'm going to go get my doll and bring her in bed with us. I think she could use some love, too!" As she scrambled out of bed to retrieve the doll, Donna's husband stirred.

"What's going on?" he asked. "Is everything OK?"

Donna nodded. "Oh yes. You know, I think I'll know I'm successful as a parent if anyone could stop either of our children and ask them 'What do your parents like about you?' and they could tell them. I'm practicing my encouragement skills on Kelsey, but as soon as Jack wakes up, I'm going to start practicing with him, too."

Her husband reached out and hugged her. "Hey, maybe we should practice encouraging each other, too."

Kelsey was scurrying back under the covers with her favorite doll. Donna was surprised to hear her talking to the doll.

"Hey, Annie, do you know what I like about you?" Kelsey was saying.

Donna shook her head in amazement. How could she have forgotten what wonderful kids she had? *I'm going to keep reminding myself,* she vowed. *And I'm going to keep reminding them, too!*

Recognize the Strength

Children, especially siblings, fight, and they often fight with words. They don't seem naturally to want to say encouraging things to each other. As parents, we have to model encouragement. The good news is that because they are young and flexible, they learn quickly how to speak words of encouragement to each other. Donna's method may be one that works for you.

Focus on Accountability

Parents simply cannot tolerate children speaking disparagingly to each other. Allowed to continue, they will grow up to be sarcastic and argumentative. Often children talk the way they do because that's what they hear from their parents all day long. So the first accountability must be on the parents' part. If we change our verbal communication with our children, we can teach them how to be encouraging and appreciative of one another.

~ 46 ~

Not Always Ready to Assemble

Ten-year-old David Hall was surrounded by birthday gifts. Amid the wrapping paper strewn everywhere and remnants of the party that had just disbanded, David's dad found him sitting quietly in front of the box containing the coveted electric train set.

"Hey, sport," he said. "You finally got that train set!"

David nodded without enthusiasm. "There sure are a lot of pieces," he observed.

His dad sat down beside him and pulled a large white sheet out of the box. "Well, the good thing is that all those pieces come with instructions," he said. "Let's get started."

It only took David a few minutes to get completely frustrated with the whole process of assembling the train.

"I *hate* this!" he exclaimed.

"Whoa, there," his dad said. "You're the one who's been asking for this for *months!*"

David frowned. "Well, I didn't know I'd have to put it *together!* I'm no good at this kind of stuff! I just want to *play* with it. I don't want to have to figure out how every piece fits."

David's dad thought for a moment. "Well, not everyone enjoys following directions, that's for sure. But sometimes you have to work hard to get what you really want."

"But I *am* willing to work hard, Dad. I'll work even *harder* doing chores if *you'll* just put this dumb train set together for me!"

His dad grinned. "Now that's not a bad idea! I'm pretty good at putting things together with a set of instructions, and you're pretty good at making things work once they're assembled. We could make a great team!"

David leaped to his feet. "I'll help you put this train together if you'll tell me what I should do, Dad."

"OK, son. You keep an eye on the lid of the box and keep reminding me what it's supposed to look like!"

Recognize the Strength

Although he is still very young, David recognizes that following detailed directions causes him great frustration. He also realizes that he can't get by with just giving up and quitting. With the help of his dad, David is beginning to recognize how he can use his strength to complement his dad's and together they form a more effective team.

Focus on Accountability

Global, big-picture learners can be recognized quickly when it comes to assembling a pile of parts. They don't read the directions. They usually just look at the picture of the completed project, study the pile of pieces for a few minutes, and then begin assembling in a way that makes sense in their mind. It doesn't even occur to them to read the directions until they discover leftover pieces. There may be times in life when they must read directions, beginning at number one and proceeding in a logical fashion. It is most helpful if they can work alongside someone who is better at the step-by-step approach. Even talking through the directions and watching while someone else does the assembly, can make the most complex project more tolerable.

∼ 47 ∼

Potty Training: Who's Training Whom?

"Sam, how about we buy big boy underwear today?" Marge Hanover sounded hopeful, but her three-year-old son firmly shook his head.

"No! I don't *want* big boy underwear!" Sam headed down the toy aisle, avoiding his mother's grasp. Marge rolled her eyes at her mother, who was shopping with her.

"Mom, what am I going to do? I can't enroll Sam in preschool until he's potty trained. He doesn't show any interest at *all!*"

Her mom nodded sympathetically, but before she could reply, Marge went on.

"And don't tell me that he won't go to college in diapers! That's *not* comforting! He's three years old—shouldn't he at least be *thinking* about getting out of diapers? Most of my friends' toddlers are way past this!"

Her mom smiled. "Now don't let *that* bother you. Every child is different, even when it comes to potty training. You'll just have to figure out what motivates Sam."

Marge was exasperated. "Mom, I've tried *everything*. I've bribed him with every toy imaginable. He shows great interest in getting the toy until he figures out what it will cost him. I've tried making him feel bad, telling him that he's just being a baby, but that doesn't seem to bother him, either. I tell him how many of his friends don't wear diapers anymore, but the peer pressure doesn't matter to him. I've been trying like mad to potty-train him for the past *year*. What's it going to take?"

Margie's mom watched Sam as he played with several of the toys on the bottom shelf. Then she turned to her daughter.

"Do you really want to know?" she asked.

Marge looked surprised. "Mother, of *course* I want to know! This is making me *crazy!*"

Her mom continued. "I think it's too important to you. I think Sam knows that, too, and he's enjoying the ability to exercise some control over *you* for once. He's a great kid, Marge. He's not really trying to irritate you. But I *do* think he enjoys being able to get a predictable reaction when he says or does certain things that bother you."

Marge considered her mother's advice. "But it *is* important to me," she objected. "It's my job to teach him how to use the toilet like a big boy."

Her mother shook her head. "No, dear, it's your job to help him grow and develop *normally*. That's different for each child. He needs your love and acceptance more than your instructions at this point. Don't waste time arguing over potty training when you could be spending it enjoying your son and strengthening your relationship."

Marge scooped Sam up and put him back in the shopping cart. "So you think I should just back off?" she asked her mom.

"I think you should let Sam know how much he means to you, and how special he is—just the way he is now. He knows what you want when it comes to potty training, and he knows what to do. Let him decide when to do it."

Marge sighed. "That's not going to be easy," she admitted. Her mother agreed.

"But dear, it eventually works itself out, believe me."

Marge stopped and looked at her mother.

"By the way, how did you get *me* potty trained when I was little?" she asked. Her mother grinned and winked at her.

"You don't want to know!"

Recognize the Strength

This is a battle of wills. Both Marge and Sam are determined in very different ways. Sam's determination not to use the potty is most annoying to his mother. Some day, though, Sam's determination will be very helpful as he grows to be an independent thinker.

Focus on Accountability

Often, as adults, we want our children to develop more quickly than they are ready to develop. This is usually because whatever they are doing causes us inconvenience. Some kids may respond to bribing, others to rationalization. Almost every child, however, responds to having a parent "back off." When we stop pressuring children, and let them exert control over their own bodies, they will learn. It will happen in its own time.

~ 48 ~

I Want to Get Dressed by Myself

"Trevor! Time to get dressed!" Barbara Nelson called to her four-year-old son for the third time. She had laid his clothes neatly on her bed so he could jump out of the bathtub and quickly get dressed for his first day of preschool.

Trevor called back from his bedroom instead of the bathroom.

"I *already* got dressed, Mommy. I did it myself!"

Barbara groaned. "Oh, no! Not *today!*" Her husband, Jeff, walked out of the master bathroom.

"What's up?" he asked.

"Of *all* days!" Barbara exclaimed. "Trevor insisted on dressing himself today. He never chooses clothes that match. Half the time they don't even fit."

Just then, Trevor bounded into the room, proudly displaying his wardrobe choice. The well-worn green pants created quite a splash under the now too-small shirt with bright red dinosaurs.

"Trevor!" cried his mother. "You can't wear *that* to school, sweetie! Let's change into *these* nice clothes." As she picked up the new clothes from the bed, she already knew it wasn't going to work. Trevor frowned and folded his arms.

"No!" he said loudly. "I like *these* clothes!" Barbara felt her frustration level rising quickly. Jeff reached over and swept Trevor into his arms.

"Tell you what, sport, you look pretty wild, but I sure like those green pants. I wonder if you and I could find another shirt you like that would look good with those pants? We'll keep these red dinosaurs for you to change into after school. What do you say?"

Trevor kept frowning, but allowed Daddy to take him back into his room for another try at a matching ensemble. When they

154

emerged, Barbara hugged them both. Trevor still looked pretty ragged, but his muted green shirt was tucked in, and he proudly wore his new super-hero tennis shoes.

"I can live with it," Barbara told Jeff. "Thanks for the rescue."

"May I make a suggestion that might seem kind of obvious?" Jeff asked. Barbara nodded.

"Well, I know you've been terribly busy and haven't had time to go through Trevor's closet and dresser drawers. But what if all three of us sorted through his clothes and took out everything that doesn't fit or won't match with certain things? Then, whenever he wants to go choose his own outfits, at least we'll know he'll be choosing from the right items in the first place."

Barbara smiled and gave him a playful punch in the arm. "Now, why didn't *I* think of that?" she said. "Let's do it tonight. Trevor will have great fun pulling out some of his favorite *little boy* clothes!"

"Time to go, Mommy!" Trevor called from the hallway.

Barbara took a deep breath. "OK, I guess I'll just have to be the mom who can't dress her kid very well today."

Jeff chuckled. "I have a feeling you won't be the *only* one who had this problem."

Barbara took Trevor's hand. "I'll bet you're right!" she called back over her shoulder.

Recognize the Strength

This little guy is an independent thinker and is taking early responsibility for himself. Give him some credit for the initiative of getting dressed on his own, as well as for the decisions he is making.

Focus on Accountability

Make sure that when a child disagrees with you, he does it in a manner that is appropriate to your family's standard of behavior. Disagreements with toddlers and preschoolers are often caused by our giving them choices or allowing them to make decisions they are not able to make. When we give them a choice, and we don't like the option they select, we can almost always count on a battle. Mrs. Nelson failed to realize that Trevor's dresser drawers contained clothing she deemed inappropriate. By leaving the clothing in the drawer for his free choice, she was asking for a problem to occur. If the child has a choice of clothing, or assumes that choice even if you have other clothes laid out, try to give him credit for decision making, without making a value judgment of what makes a good "clothing match."

∼ 49 ∼

Who Gets to Win the Battle of Wills?

She had read "just one more story" to her six-year-old daughter Alicia. Theresa Evans was ready to call it a night. Alicia had gone through her whole routine of stalling, begging for more time, and actively arguing about why sleep was necessary in the first place. Theresa was just about completely worn out, but Alicia seemed determined to stay up just a little longer. Finally, Mom laid down the law.

"Alicia, good night. Go to sleep, and I'll see you in the morning." She kissed Alicia's cheek, tucked her between the sheets, turned out the light, and turned to leave the room. Determined to at least have the last word, Alicia called after her mom.

"Mom, leave the hall light on."

Theresa replied, "No, sweetheart, we're not going to leave the hall light on."

"Yes, I want the hall light on."

"No. No hall light."

"Yes."

"No."

"Yes."

"No," and the hall light went off.

Alicia began to cry. Theresa frowned, and decided her strong-willed daughter could jolly well cry herself to sleep.

Two hours later, both of them were sick of it. Alicia was tired of crying, but she wasn't about to give in. Her mom was tired of listening, but it had been decided that the hall light was *not* going to go on.

Finally Theresa walked back down the hall, looked in to discover Alicia had uncovered one of her feet from the blanket. The teary-eyed little girl said, "Mom, if you'll cover my foot up I'll go to sleep."

So her mom covered Alicia's foot and the exhausted little girl went to sleep. Theresa smiled and shook her head as she left Alicia's room. *Well,* she thought, *Alicia may have decided the war was no longer worth winning, but obviously unconditional surrender was out of the question!*

Theresa had maintained her authority as a parent, but the compromise had allowed Alicia a graceful way to surrender the battle.

Recognize the Strength

This little girl has a strong-willed nature; she will challenge on many issues. Recognize that she is constantly thinking, willing to speak her mind confidently and capably, and that throughout her life she will stand firm for what she believes to be fair and true. She will become a leader rather than a follower of her peers.

Focus on Accountability

The battle of wills is a tough challenge for many parents and teachers. For young children like Alicia, immaturity is the cause of many battles. As we have said before, choose your battles. Ask yourself, "Is this battle worth fighting? Will it matter weeks or months from now who wins this one?" If you believe leaving the hall light on is worth fighting for, then enter the battle. However, if you determine *sleep* is the issue and it doesn't matter if the hall light is on or off, then don't make it an issue. If leaving the hall light on will induce sleep, perhaps that is the choice to make.

~ 50 ~

How Will I Know I'm Special?

Bobby ran over to his teacher, Miss Milnes. "I got the right answer! Can I stamp a smiley face on my hand?"

"Sure, Bobby. Please work quietly while others finish their work," she said in her patient way. Miss Milnes enjoyed being a second-grade teacher. The children were so full of energy and so eager to learn. They were a constant inspiration to her.

Later in the day, as she was returning some math papers, Bobby started wildly waving his arm in the air. "Miss Milnes, Miss Milnes, did you put stickers on our papers today?"

"Not this time, Bobby. I'll save them for another important assignment," she said, knowing he would be disappointed.

"Ohhh, pleeese can we have stickers?" Bobby pleaded.

Miss Milnes had repositioned herself nearer to Bobby's desk. She leaned over and whispered, "If you bring it up to my desk a little later, I'll put a gold star on it just for you."

Bobby ran out the door to recess not remembering to get his gold star. After recess, the children gathered around the big overstuffed chair for show and tell.

"Who would like to share today?" Miss Milnes asked.

Several hands went up cautiously, and several more were waving and saying, "Me! Me! Me!" As the children took their turns, each received a sticker on their shirt that made a proclamation of *Keep it Up, Well Done, Nice Job*. Miss Milnes kept a secret list of whom she had called on, so that everyone had an equal number of times to share, and no one was accidentally left out.

On his way out the door at the end of the day, Bobby looked at Miss Milnes and pouted, "I didn't get a sticker on my shirt because you didn't let me share today."

Miss Milnes crouched down next to Bobby so she was only as tall as he was. She looked into his downcast little face and said, "I don't need to give you a special sticker for everything, or even a special sticker just for sharing. You are special every day and in every way. Will you remember that for me?"

His face beamed. "Do you mean that? Do you really mean I'm special every day?"

"Yes, I do. In fact, our special sign to each other from now on is going to be a thumbs-up. We're going to talk about it tomorrow morning when we start class. You're the only one to know about it today. It can be our secret tonight. When I see something I appreciate or like you doing or saying, I'll give you a thumbs-up. Okay?" Miss Milnes demonstrated for him. "Can you do it back to me?"

"Sure can," Bobby said as he ran out the door.

Recognize the Strength

Needing a tangible reward for everything they do may be the only source of motivation developed in some people. Bobby knows his need, and his teacher is working at broadening his idea about what it will take to motivate him.

Focus on Accountability

The need for an external, tangible reward for the work one does is an extrinsic form of motivation. These types of rewards can very easily be met for some children, especially in the preschool years and early grade levels. Stickers, stamps, trinkets, and even grades or points help young children see and appreciate the value of learning and completing their work. At home, an allowance or special privilege is often the extrinsic motivator. Try also to develop some forms of *intrinsic* motivators for children. A sense of accomplishment, being told "Job Well Done," the "thumbs up" signal, a pat on the back, or just knowing he did his best can be forms of intrinsic motivation that work for many children. The type of motivator they need, intrinsic or extrinsic, may in part be influenced by their learning style. Exposing them to lots of variety will help them learn what works best for them, and will help them know how to help *themselves* when parents and teachers aren't looking after them anymore.

~ 51 ~

I Need to Know the Right Answer

Alicia had always been a good student. Her freshman year of high school, however, had brought a few new challenges. Alicia was careful to come to school prepared, with plenty of paper, pens, and necessary school supplies. She listened carefully to her teachers, and followed their instructions to the letter. Most teachers loved the way she paid such close attention to every detail and the way she followed directions quickly and accurately. Her grades reflected her conscientious efforts. Imagine her surprise, then, when she enrolled in her freshman literature class and encountered a teacher who was nothing like she had yet seen in her solid, predictable life.

Mr. Willis described himself as *creative*. Alicia thought he bordered on *crazy*. He often came dressed in mismatched shirt and pants, and frequently stopped in the middle of a lecture to tell a totally unrelated joke or story. He described his teaching style as *passionate*, but Alicia thought it was more like *scatterbrained*. Mr. Willis claimed he was trying to teach his students to think, but Alicia was sure he was trying to drive her stark raving mad.

"Mr. Willis doesn't even finish some of his sentences!" she complained to her mom. "He doesn't think it matters if you finish something as long as you have the general idea." Alicia was especially worried about her grades. She had a hard time pinning Mr. Willis down to describing the grading scale.

"How much is this essay worth?" she would ask him. He would smile and get that faraway look she dreaded.

"Well, Alicia, that essay is only worth the effort and thought you put into it. In other words, what's it worth *to you?*"

Although she had survived the first three weeks of Mr. Willis' class, the final straw was the day he had the entire class read Frank

Stockton's short story *The Lady or the Tiger*. The story itself seemed pretty straightforward to Alicia. The princess had fallen in love with her chauffeur, and they had been caught. As punishment, her lover must now open one of two doors. Behind one door is a ferocious tiger who will instantly kill him. Behind the other door is the most beautiful woman in the land who will marry him. Either way, the princess is doomed to lose her love. He knows she will find out what lies behind each door and will be able to direct his choice. Before he makes his choice, he looks at her and she signals him. He opens the door she has chosen for him, and it is....

Alicia can't believe it. There's no *ending*? "Yes, yes!" cries Mr. Willis gleefully. Isn't it invigorating just to consider all the possibilities? Alicia is thoroughly disgusted. "Expand your horizons!" shouts Mr. Willis. Think of the complexities of this problem! Let your mind toy with creative solutions!

Alicia raised her hand. "Mr. Willis, what ending did Mr. *Stockton* write?"

Mr. Willis seemed surprised at the question.

"Why, Alicia, he didn't *write* one. He left that up to our imaginations!"

Alicia lost all patience.

"Mr. Willis, please call him up. Or give me his number and *I'll* call him. He has to tell us how he wanted his story to end!"

Mr. Willis frowned. Obviously Alicia had missed the point.

"My dear child," he said, "Mr. Stockton has been dead for many years. We'll *never* know what his ending would have been."

Alicia felt so angry she was close to tears. She had never felt so much like talking back to a teacher. This was so unfair!

Mr. Willis seemed to sense her frustration.

"Alicia, I know this is frustrating to those who simply want pat answers. And there's a lot to be said for having certain unchangeable solutions to life's everyday problems. But my job is to help you learn to deal with people like *me!* If you think I irritate you, wait until you graduate and enter the world of diversity! Perhaps it would be easier for you to get along in this class if you just considered me as your on-the-job-training."

Alicia felt herself smile. That was so ridiculous! And yet, Mr. Willis didn't seem to be mad at her or anything. As long as he *knew* how irritating it was for her to deal with his vague generalities and calls to use her imagination, maybe she could put up with his unusual class requirements.

Alicia sighed and pulled out a clean sheet of paper. Now let's see, if *she* were the princess...

Recognize the Strength

Alicia is the type of student who likes everything to be black and white, cut and dried, sequential and logical, a definite answer or conclusion. Children like Alicia will find many avenues to demonstrate these skills, and they are very decisive and confident in the decisions they make.

Focus on Accountability

Creativity and the land of assumptions and what-ifs is a very scary place for students like Alicia. When the world is gray, and there are no lines to color inside of, children like Alicia will try to create their own limitations so they feel more comfortable. In the unfinished work of Frank Stockton, a creative ending to the story is a real stretch for Alicia. However, the parameters have been laid in the story. Alicia just needs to realize that she has a starting place and only needs to arrange the details of the ending to her liking. She must realize that not having a published ending doesn't excuse her from completing the story Mr. Willis has requested.

∼ 52 ∼

Can You Pass the Test
without Doing the Homework?

Mrs. Roberts was shocked to get a notice from Sarah's teacher, Miss Patton, that said Sarah was failing in math. Sarah was a bright, capable, and ambitious fifth-grader who had excelled in math during the first half of the year. Her mom was determined to get to the bottom of the problem, and she and Sarah went to discuss the situation with Miss Patton.

Miss Patton graciously ushered Sarah and her mother into the small conference room and answered Mrs. Roberts' first and most obvious question: *What happened?*

"Sarah suddenly decided to quit doing her math homework," Miss Patton said. "Homework counts for a substantial portion of the semester grade, and now Sarah's normally excellent academic record is in trouble."

Mrs. Roberts turned to her daughter. "Sarah, why aren't you turning in your homework? I thought you *loved* math!"

"I *do* love math," Sarah replied. "But the homework's too *boring*. I hate having to do twenty problems when I understand how to do the process after doing five of them. I just decided it wasn't worth the trouble."

Miss Patton didn't seem to be bothered by the criticism. She turned and looked at Sarah intently.

"Do you think you can pass the math tests without doing all the homework?" she asked.

"Oh sure," Sarah replied. "I always get As on my tests."

Miss Patton looked at Sarah's mom. "Sarah does get good grades on her tests," she admitted. "I just haven't made any exceptions on the homework grades."

After some discussion among Sarah, her mother, and Miss Patton, they came up with what they thought might be a workable solution. Sarah agreed to do at least half of her homework every night. If she got a 92 percent or better on her math test, her teacher would give her full credit for the homework assignments. If she got lower than 92 percent, she would agree to complete whichever assignments her teacher deemed necessary.

Sarah kept her end of the bargain. Some nights she did *more* than half of the homework, because now she knew she was only doing what she needed in order to master the concept. She never did fall below a 92 percent on any math test the rest of the year. Not only that, she taught her parents and her teacher there are many reasons why a child might fail in an assignment and many ways to achieve the desired results.

Recognize the Strength

For a child like Sarah, life is constantly moving forward. Because she is strong-willed, she would take a zero before doing a job that she believed was unnecessary. For children like Sarah, we must appreciate that she knows herself well enough to recognize when she has mastered a concept and when more work is needed. She has a strength of conviction that will help her stand against peer pressure.

Focus on Accountability

Perhaps this is a good lesson for everyone. Try to determine what individual children need in order to learn. Sarah knew when she had done enough problems to cement her new learning. Your child may simply be more compliant and do what he or she is told, regardless of the number of problems in the assignment. But for students like Sarah, five problems instead of twenty is enough. The accountability in this case fell into the lap of both the teacher and the student. How much do you need to do to pass the test? Once the criteria is determined, and Sarah could demonstrate the 92 percent score, then the volume of homework could be adjusted to meet her particular needs. Helping Sarah monitor her own level of practice was a way for her to be in control and accountable for the outcome.

∼ 53 ∼

Could You Be More Specific?

"Mrs. Jacobs, what did I get on my test?"

The harried sixth-grade teacher looked over at Sally Tate. "Did I forget to put your score at the top of the paper? Sorry."

Sally shook her head. "It says 88 percent. But I don't know what that means. Is it an *A* or a *B* or a *C*?"

Mrs. Jacobs seemed preoccupied. "It's a good score, Sally. Your work is improving. Keep it up!"

Sally persisted. "But Mrs. Jacobs, what *grade* did I get?"

Mrs. Jacobs was becoming a little impatient. "Sally, I'd have to look it up on the grade scale. Could you check with me later?"

Sally left reluctantly. Mrs. Jacobs sighed. She tried not to let students get to her, but Sally was beginning to be very annoying. It seemed like she had to know every little detail about her grades.

"Mrs. Jacobs?" It was Sally again.

"What is it, Sally?"

"On this essay we're turning in, you said to write two or three ideas about why we need to get involved in politics. Do you want two reasons, or three reasons?"

Mrs. Jacobs couldn't hide her exasperation. "Oh, Sally, for goodness sake. You decide. Two *or* three will be fine."

Sally wasn't satisfied. "Would I get a better grade if I did three?"

"No." Mrs. Jacobs' answer was swift and abrupt. Sally looked hurt.

"I was just asking," she said quickly.

Mrs. Jacobs stopped what she was doing and turned to Sally.

"Sally, I'm sorry. I have to admit I get a little frustrated when you ask me all these detailed questions."

"I'm sorry, Mrs. Jacobs," Sally replied. "My dad is really picky about my grades and everything, and I have to tell him how I'm doing every day. A lot of times, I just don't know."

Mrs. Jacobs smiled, "I know grades are important to you, especially since you want your dad to know you're doing well. It's just less complicated for me if I put everything in percentages. Then I can average the scores quickly."

Sally nodded. "It's OK, Mrs. Jacobs. I didn't want to make you do extra work."

Mrs. Jacobs smiled at Sally's thoughtfulness.

"Hey, I'll tell you what," she said. "What if I make you a copy of my grading scale? You can tape it inside your notebook and then figure out what each of your percentage scores means."

Sally's face brightened.

"That would be great! Maybe my dad would like to have a copy too, and then he could figure out the grades for himself!!"

Mrs. Jacobs reached out and patted Sally's arm.

"Sally, I'll try to give you more detailed information, then you can be prepared to explain your work to your dad. But you may have to remind me once in a while that you need me to be more specific."

"Oh, no, Mrs. Jacobs. I couldn't do that. You're a great teacher. I'll just write down that scale, and then I won't have to bother you."

Mrs. Jacobs shook her head. "You're not bothering me, Sally. I just need to remember that I'm not the only one teaching the lessons here."

Recognize the Strength

Sally is learning about dependability and accountability. She is also showing the ability to follow through with the request from Dad to document progress. These are solid character traits that develop early in some children.

Focus on Accountability

Sally, in her quiet, thoughtful way, was carefully and politely seeking bits of information that would help her provide a logical and sequential analysis for her dad of her work and grades. Dad is teaching Sally about accountability so she, in turn, is holding the teacher accountable. This child and those like her appreciate others who hold to their word, who are dependable and trustworthy. These are all values that are highly marketable when seeking employment or career opportunities.

~ 54 ~

Are You Sure This Is Just Sibling Rivalry?

"You're such a geek!"

Although Josh's voice was changing because of adolescence, it was at least an octave higher due to rage. His ten-year-old brother, Steve, glared at him in anger.

"I saw it first," he insisted, "and I can't help it if there's only one." They were standing together in the aisle of the toy store, and their mother was headed toward them fast.

"Boys! I can hear you way down at the other end of the store! What in the world is the problem?"

Twelve-year-old Josh shook his fist at Steve. "My stupid brother grabbed the last one! I saved my money for it and this geek snagged it right out from under my nose."

Steve stuck out his tongue. "I didn't see your *name* on it, Bozo." Josh pulled his hand back to hit his brother. His mom grabbed his arm.

"That's enough!" she exclaimed. "This is *ridiculous* to come to blows over some silly toy."

"He does this all the time, Mom," Josh complained. "It's like he tries to figure out what I want just so *he* can get to it first."

"Well, no one gets it this time," Mom said firmly. She took the box from Steve, returned it to the shelf, and marched both boys out to the car.

"Way to go," Josh muttered to Steve. "Now we don't get anything."

Steve fumed, "You're the one who made it such a big deal. You're a jerk."

"I am not!" exclaimed Josh.

"Are, too."

"Am not."

"Are, too."

"That's it!" Now Mom was almost screaming. "I can't stand it any more! We are going straight home and I'm calling your aunt in Cleveland to see if she and I can take turns having just *one* of you at a time."

Both boys looked startled.

"OK, I'm kidding," admitted Mom. "At least I think I'm kidding. But I just don't understand why the two of you can't get along. You used to love to play together. Steve, you used to think having a big brother was great."

"Yeah, well that was before I knew he was going to turn out to be so dumb."

"Stephen Richards, I *never* want to hear you calling people names—especially not your own brother."

"Yeah," Josh echoed, "why would you say that?"

Steve reached over and punched his brother's arm, and the wrestling match began.

Fortunately, they were pulling into their driveway and Mrs. Richards stopped the car.

"Boys! I'm serious. If you don't stop *right now*, I'll hose you both down while you're still in the car."

Josh and Steve scrambled outside and chased each other into the house.

Mrs. Richards' neighbor was sitting on his porch, observing the skirmish. Mr. Peters was in his eighties now, but everyone enjoyed his keen wit and wise insights.

She waved at him and he motioned her over.

"Having a bad day?" he asked her.

"Are you kidding? Lately every day has been like this. I must not be a very good mother for boys. I think they're going to kill each other before they reach high school."

Mr. Peters chuckled. "Well, now, maybe that's what you should be worried most about—that they don't kill each other. After all, boys will be boys."

Mrs. Richards shook her head. "That's just an excuse. If you can't be nice to your own brother, how can you learn to be good to others?"

Mr. Peters leaned forward, "Well, do you want them to practice on strangers or on each other? You do have to draw a few hard lines, but your boys are good kids. They won't argue forever, and they can help each other figure out where the boundaries are, and when one of them has stepped over the line."

Mrs. Richards sighed. "Are you saying I should back off?" she asked.

"Oh, don't let them get by with much," said Mr. Peters, "but don't panic about why they start arguing and fighting and name-calling. At least they're comfortable enough with each other to say how they feel. Lots of families don't talk to one another at all."

"Mr. Peters, you're a wise man."

He grunted. "Sure took me long enough."

"Do you have a brother?" she asked.

Mr. Peters nodded and winked. "Passed on before me. That ornery cuss was bound and determined to do everything first."

Recognize the Strength

A battle of the wills among siblings is common to every household with more than one child. Siblings are practicing on each other the negotiating skills they will put to good use as adults. Josh and Steve are practicing expressing their opinions, jockeying for a position of leadership, checking out what it's like to be determined, and standing their ground for what they believe is just and fair.

Focus on Accountability

Although listening to and watching the quarreling that turns daily routines into chaos may drive you to distraction, remember it is forward progress. As the immaturity of childhood gives way to the turbulent years of adolescence and the maturing years of adulthood, the friendship that grows slowly between siblings through the sometimes fierce battling will become the solid foundation of a friendship that lasts into the final years of life.

～ 55 ～

This Vacation Is Boring

"I'm bored! We never do anything fun on vacation!"

Gail Barton looked at her ten-year-old daughter, Allison, who wore an exaggerated expression of pain.

"Allison Barton, that's not true! We've just spent three days on the beach doing only what you and your brothers wanted to do. You've been horseback riding, clam digging, moped riding, and shopping."

"Yeah, but it's still been boring," she insisted. "I want something exciting to do."

Her mother looked at her. "Allison, I'm not sure there's anything in the world that is exciting enough for you. I've never seen anyone with a greater sense of adventure and exploration."

Allison brightened. "Could we go explore something?" she asked hopefully.

Her mother frowned in concentration. "We'll talk to your father, but this little beach town is not exactly the center of dark mystery or scientific discovery."

"See?" replied Allison. "We never go anywhere fun!"

Her father stepped into the room. "Hey, I couldn't help but over-hear our little girl complaining about my choice of vacation spots. Allie, I thought you'd love this place!"

"It's all the same," explained Allison. "I want something different."

"Like what?" her father asked.

"I don't know!" she exclaimed. "But there has to be something that no one has thought of before!"

Her dad looked at her for a moment. "Well then, why don't you try thinking of it? You're always coming up with new ideas. Why not see if you can think of something exciting we could do here at the beach?"

Allison looked frustrated. Her mom stepped forward. "We could help you get started, if you like. Your brothers are fishing. Do you want to wait for them to begin an adventure, or should you and I go on and find some excitement on our own?"

Allison didn't want to wait, so she and her mom sat down in the kitchen area of the beach cabin while Dad took off to join her brothers.

Gail pulled out a clean sheet of paper and a pen. "Allison, the way I figure, we can spend about $20 today between the two of us and not put a crimp in our vacation fund. Your dad and brothers will want to join us for dinner in about four hours. Let's just brainstorm a few things we could do for that amount of money and time."

After a few minutes of wild ideas—finding the nearest prison, adopting an abandoned seagull, and lots more—Allison and her mom had two or three leads that held the promise of new, unexplored territory, including visiting the local newspaper and the town hall. Allison was sure this town had a secret, and she was bound to find it. Gail was immensely relieved to find a way to engage her daughter's active mind while still being able to control most of the circumstances.

Recognize the Strength

Allison is an innovative, cutting-edge, creative thinker who just needs a problem to solve. If you are a parent or teacher of this type of child, try to provide a situation for him or her to put these skills to work for the benefit of the whole family.

Focus on Accountability

Helping Allison take responsibility for her boredom is the beginning of the solution. By getting her to buy into the solution, she becomes part of it. Allison was able to find the solutions that met the criteria her mother laid out. Let the adventure-seeking child, who always wants to be on the go, tackle the problem of finding something to do. Let the child come up with a creative solution. Handing the problem to the child to solve, rather than solving it for him or her, is a great way for the child to practice problem-solving skills.

~ 56 ~

We Can't Keep Every Stray Animal

"Mommy, can we keep him?" Jimmy Mason stood outside the front door, hugging a damp and distinctly odorous small dog. Jane Mason looked at her seven-year-old son in dismay.

"Oh Jimmy, not another one! You already have a dog, two cats, three birds, a hamster, and three fish."

"But Mom, this dog really needs me!" His eyes were pleading. Jane hesitated. She always tried to tread easily when it came to dealing with her youngest son's tender heart. Jimmy was by far the most sensitive member of the family, and he was constantly looking for ways to help anyone who seemed to be the underdog. Well, this time he had certainly found an underdog!

She sighed and let the two of them in. "Go straight to the laundry room," she instructed Jimmy. "I'll bring you some soap so you can give that dog a bath. When he's clean, we'll need to decide what to do with him." Jimmy brightened and took off.

Later, mom and son sat at the kitchen table while the trembling stray sat in a sleeping basket borrowed from one of the cats.

"Jimmy, we can't keep another dog. We just don't have the room, and you don't have time to take care of another animal with all the chores you already have with the other animals."

"But Mom," Jimmy protested. "I can't just leave him on the street! Someone will run over him!"

"Jimmy," she replied firmly. "I know you want to take care of anyone and anything that needs help. You have a very good heart, but there are limits. You don't have the time and we don't have the money for food for another animal. We have to find another solution."

Jimmy looked stricken. "But Mom, they all need me! I can't stop being nice to the animals I find that need me!"

Mom looked at her son's crestfallen face. "Hey, don't look so sad. We're not going to just dump him out on the street. Here's an idea. How about you and I write a newspaper ad for the Lost and Found section? We'll run the ad for three days to see if we can find his owner. Then, if no one calls, we'll contact the Humane Society and see if they can help us place the dog. During the next three or four days, you can try to learn what the dog likes, how he acts, and whether or not he gets along with our cats and other animals. Then, we'll write up a little description so the Humane Society will know how to advertise him to prospective owners. Jimmy, there are lots of people with no animals at all who would love to have this little dog. Just think how nice it would be for somebody out there to have you help them find the right animal."

Jimmy smiled. "That's a good idea! I could help people *and* animals then!"

His mother reached out and patted his arm.

"Jimmy, we need to agree that you will do this within a one week period. In the future, you can't bring in more than one stray during seven days, and you can't keep any animal for more than seven days before we find a place for it. Deal?"

Jimmy thought for a moment, then thrust out his hand. "Deal!" he said confidently. He jumped up to let one of the cats in the back door.

"Hey Mom!" he called. "Tiger has a new friend!"

Jane groaned.

"Jimmy, close the door!"

Recognize the Strength

Jimmy has a soft heart, full of compassion and empathy. Right now, it's easy for him to pour this out on stray animals. A child like Jimmy will be able to put this appreciation of others to great use as he moves through life. Soft-hearted kids like Jimmy often turn out to be doctors, social workers, ministers, and caregivers.

Focus on Accountability

It is good for Jimmy to realize that his love for stray animals causes both a financial hardship on the family budget as well as a strain on his time. By talking this over with him, pointing out how this has affected him and the family, his mom capitalized on his strength of tenderness. Jimmy now understands how one decision affects everyone around him. The child with an over-generous heart needs to work at staying within the parameters or guidelines parents set down. We do not want to squelch that generous spirit, but by defining it, it becomes more manageable.

~ 57 ~

No One Wants to Play with Me

Janice Carter was sitting anxiously in front of Brittany's preschool teacher for the first parent conference of the year. She hoped Miss Sampson had recognized that Brittany was a very intelligent and capable little girl.

"Mrs. Carter," Miss Sampson began carefully. "Brittany is extremely bright. I believe in many ways she is gifted beyond her years."

Janice beamed. Although she already knew of Brittany's intelligence, the fact that her teacher recognized it would be wonderful news to share with her husband, George, tonight!

Miss Sampson continued, "I do think we'll need to focus on at least one area where Brittany could use a little help."

Janice frowned. "What is it?" she asked.

Miss Sampson looked a little uncomfortable. "Well, Brittany already shows some real leadership abilities. Unfortunately, she insists on directing and instructing every other child on the playground. She's creating a situation where no one wants to play with her."

Janice felt her heart sink. Brittany could be quite bossy, even at home. She always seemed to have a better idea, or wanted to do things a different way. At first, she and George had thought it was cute. Now it seemed it was going to keep Brittany from having friends.

"What can we do?" Janice asked.

Miss Sampson thought for a moment. "I know that Brittany has no other siblings, so you may not have had too many chances to see how she interacts with other children. I think it would be a very good idea for both you and your husband to spend a little time observing Brittany at school, especially when she's playing with the other kids.

179

You could also have groups of children to your home for play time."

Janice nodded, and Miss Sampson continued.

"I also think that talking to Brittany will help a lot. She's very smart, and I think she's feeling hurt by the other children's rejection. I wouldn't make her feel bad about being bossy. I would just try to help her understand how it makes her classmates feel when she tells them what to do. Maybe a role play, where you play Brittany and Brittany plays another child, would serve to make her aware of what she is doing. The most important thing, I think, is to encourage her to learn how to make other children feel important, too. If Brittany can learn how to do that, her leadership skills will be virtually unlimited."

Janice smiled. "You know, we're talking about a four year old, here. Isn't she a little young to be bothered with all of this?"

Miss Sampson shook her head. "This is an ideal time to help Brittany recognize her strengths and learn how to use her interpersonal communication skills positively. Besides, every child needs to feel appreciated and accepted by others. I'd like us to help Brittany get on the right track as early as possible, so that she enters kindergarten with the skills of a leader and the friends of a diplomat."

Janice stood and shook hands with Miss Sampson. "Thanks. I have a feeling this won't be easy. Brittany is a very determined child. But I'll talk to my husband, and we'll try taking your advice. Who knows? We may find that our Brittany will someday be the leader of the free world!"

Recognize the Strength

In her immaturity, Brittany is using strong but undeveloped leadership skills in a negative way. With some guidance, Brittany and children like her can learn to be more sensitive and to share control. As time goes on, these children will become more aware that others have suggestions to offer. They will develop a leadership style that takes the needs and ideas of others into consideration.

Focus on Accountability

If you encounter children like Brittany, make sure they perceive their bossy attitude as a problem that needs to be corrected and then show them how to do it. It is important for these children to comprehend how their behavior has an impact on the thoughts and feelings of those around them. Brittany, even at four years of age, needs to understand her responsibility as a friend. Children this young can be helped by your reading to them some preschool books about friendship, and by talking casually about what it means to be a friend. As parents, encourage and nurture leadership strengths you see in your children. There has been a lot of talk in recent years about a "crisis of leadership" in our world. You could, in your home, be growing a strong leader who cares about the needs of others.

∼ 58 ∼

Isn't It Close Enough?

Andrew grabbed another copy of the *Journal* out of his paper bag, rolled it and heaved it into the Kellors' yard. Oops! It hit a shrub next to the front door, but didn't break anything. *Close enough*, he thought as he rode on. *No hands on the handlebars for the whole block—I'm getting pretty good at this.* Andrew was eleven years old, in the fifth grade, and loved his new mountain bike.

"Hi, Mrs. Daley," he said, slowing to a stop. As his foot hit the sidewalk, he grabbed his water bottle for a long drink.

"Are you working hard today?" she asked in a frail voice, as she accepted her rolled-up paper from Andrew.

"Not really. I don't consider this work. I'm just having fun on my bike," he said. "See you tomorrow."

As she shuffled back toward her house, Mrs. Daley watched Andrew ride off, no hands, and longed for the freedom of movement that arthritis had stolen from her.

Andrew continued on his route, rolling newspapers, one at a time. He would throw each paper as close to the door as he could. Not walking each paper to the porch and placing it neatly on the doormat saved a lot of time. "Close enough" was his motto, except for Mrs. Daley. He always stopped and handed the paper to her.

One evening the phone rang. He heard his dad say "I'll talk to him about it. Thank you for calling." Andrew deduced quickly that someone from his paper route was complaining. As his dad rounded the corner into the family room, Andrew braced for the bad news.

"Andrew," Mr. Dixon said in his calm manner. "That was Mrs. Blanchard from down on Madrona Street. She claims you flung the paper into her yard while riding recklessly past on your bike. When you flung the paper, it landed on top of a rhododendron bush." Mr.

Dixon looked his son in the eye and quietly asked, "Son, is this true?"

"Well, yes, but I wasn't riding recklessly, I was just riding with no hands," Andrew admitted. "But all she had to do was come out the front door and grab the paper. It was close enough. In fact, she didn't even have to lean over."

"Son, some people take great pride in the way their yards look. Some people expect things to be done in an exact way. Those kinds of people like to find the paper on the front doormat. 'Close enough' isn't part of their vocabulary," Mr. Dixon stated rather forcefully.

"But Dad, I don't have time to place it neatly on the mat, centered perfectly and parallel to the sidewalk. I aim carefully, and most of the time I really get it pretty close to where it belongs with no problems," Andrew explained, trying to justify his methodology.

"But 'pretty close' just doesn't work for some people, even if it does work for you," Mr. Dixon reminded.

"Yeah. Like Mrs. Grant." *Ugh!* thought Andrew, as it slipped out.

"What about Mrs. Grant?" his dad inquired.

"Well, she kinda has a long driveway," Andrew admitted, "so I was kinda cutting the corners and riding my bike across her grass and she keeps asking me not to do it, but I never remember until I'm already on the lawn and then it's too late." He winced, not knowing what might happen next.

In the same calm manner, Mr. Dixon asked, "Is she going to be calling, too?"

"Maybe," Andrew said looking down at his feet. "I guess some people just don't like 'close enough' do they?" After a pause, he added, "But if it works for me, why doesn't it work for everybody?"

"Because you're not everybody. You're Andrew and we love you. But we need to help you so you don't have customers calling and canceling the *Journal* because of the way you deliver it," Mr. Dixon explained.

"Would they really cancel their paper just because of me?" Andrew was surprised.

"They might," Mr. Dixon said as he and Andrew walked out the back door. "If you don't want to lose customers, perhaps you can change your philosophy, at least during your paper route. Your mother and I have accepted your 'close enough' ways because we know that's how you think. But sometimes 'close enough' isn't close enough, and sometimes others may have different ideas and expect you to change and do it their way. Does that make sense to you?"

"Close enough!" Andrew said as he rode down the driveway with no hands.

Recognize the Strength

"Close enough" is a philosophy that may be very helpful in many situations. "Close enough" helps many people enjoy a more leisurely cadence to life, focusing on the big idea or the gist of the matter without getting bogged down in the details. People with this philosophy won't be stressed out by so many things, and may have a decreased risk of heart attack because they live life at a slower, less critical pace.

Focus on the Accountability

The issue here is the treatment of other people's property. Andrew needed to realize that his attitude about "close enough" was causing frustration in his customers, and he seemed unaware that his actions might affect his paycheck. It is good for a child of Andrew's age to realize that behavior is often linked to financial benefits. Learning this lesson now will help Andrew and children with a similar philosophy make more conscious choices regarding how to carry out their responsibilities toward clients in order to keep their integrity and effectiveness.

～ 59 ～

Stay Where I Can See You

As they sat by the morning campfire, waiting for the children to wake up, Dale and Kristine talked about the day.

"What do you want to do?" Dale asked.

"How about a hike?" Kristine suggested. "Maybe we could go to the top of Cougar Ridge. Lake Wilderness is up there too. We could take a lunch in the day pack."

"Sounds great to me," Dale said, sipping some hot coffee.

After bacon and pancakes cooked over the fire, everyone had plenty of energy to get started.

The trail was steep from the very beginning. Amanda and Amy, the seven-year-old twins, ran way ahead, then walked back to meet everyone, then ran way ahead again. It was a game to them. Dale and the two boys, Thomas aged ten and Jonathan aged fourteen, were involved in a discussion about fly fishing.

"I want to have trout for dinner. When can we go fishing, Dad?" Thomas asked.

"We shouldn't eat the fish," Jonathan pondered, "or we won't have anything to fish for pretty soon. I really think the catch-and-release idea that Grandpa is promoting is a good idea. If you stop to think about it and weigh the pros and cons, I think you'll agree with me."

"You've got a point, son," Dale said, admiring Jonathan, who was now as tall as he was.

"Please, Dad, can we go fishing and catch some fish for dinner?" Thomas begged.

With only minor huffing and puffing, they broke out of the trees and as they reached the top of the ridge, the lake spread out before them, surrounded by a beautiful alpine meadow filled with wild flowers. It was postcard perfect. With lunch to refresh them, they were ready for the afternoon. After skipping some rocks, wading their toes in the icy cold lake water, and catching a few salamanders, Kristine and the girls decided to hike back down to camp.

"You'll be all right?" Dale asked.

"Yes, the trail is easy to follow and there's no way we can get lost. How long before you come back?" Kristine asked the boys.

"We're just going to explore around the lake," Thomas said.

"We should be back near five o'clock. We'll be pretty hungry by then," Dale said, checking his watch.

After reminders to be careful, the girls went downhill and the guys headed around the lake.

Jonathan, in his typical analytic, debate-all-the-options way of thinking, was still arguing about the fishing issue. Thomas had given up ever getting his point across, so he had wandered over to some rocks and was climbing around hunting for "gold." Dale decided to lay in the grass and catch a couple winks of sleep.

"Dad, Jonathan and I want to go up in that grassy area and explore. Is that OK?" Thomas called.

"Sure, I'll be there in a few minutes," Dale said with his eyes closed.

The boys ran up the slope. As Dale drifted off to sleep, the boys wandered further and further from the lake until they slipped out of sight. After nearly an hour, Dale was startled awake by a screeching hawk. The boys were nowhere to be seen. He quickly headed closer to the lake, yelling for the boys, with no response. Starting to feel desperate, he continued his search for Thomas and Jonathan, debating the options while reprimanding himself for falling asleep. At 4:30 he decided to head back down, hoping the boys had returned to camp.

His steps hastened as he spotted Kristine and the twins near the creek. "Are the boys far behind? I have dinner ready," Kristine smiled.

"No." Dale looked at her. He quickly explained what happened and then said, "I'll find the ranger, and then I'll head back up to the lake. We still have three hours of daylight."

The next three hours were painful as Kristine tried not to let her panic show. Finally at 10:00 P.M., with only a glimmer of daylight left in the west, the boys wandered into camp just off the trail, very tired and hungry. Jonathan explained every detail about how they got lost and how they analyzed every minute detail to determine how to get down off the ridge. "We must have been walking parallel to the trail all the way down. We were so close to it!" Jonathan laughed.

"Sometimes you drive me crazy the way you analyze everything," admitted Kristine. "But after today, I am so thankful you have that ability." The lump in her throat was too large to continue.

Dale thanked the ranger, and then added, "Son, those analytic skills are going to help you climb bigger mountains than Cougar Ridge. You're going to conquer whatever mountain you encounter."

Recognize the Strength

The analytic skills Jonathan used to help him make deductions and come to conclusions about his location and how to return to safety, combined with his calm and collected emotions, proved to be life-saving in this situation. These same abilities are highly valued in the business community, in either corporate positions or those of public service such as policemen or firemen.

Focus on Accountability

By wandering away from their dad, Jonathan and Thomas put themselves in danger. It is often difficult for children to realize the impact of what appears on the surface to be a minor infraction, such as staying together in the wilderness. Talking through their behavior and the possible consequences undoubtedly helped these two boys realize their error in judgment. Planning ahead and anticipating possible dangers may have prevented this event from occurring.

The boys needed to maintain contact with an adult in any type of hiking or mountaineering experience. As young men, they perhaps were unaware of the danger they placed themselves in by wandering away. Always keeping an adult informed of their whereabouts, whether at home or any alternative location, is important for health and safety reasons. When taking children or young adults on vacations to forest locations, make sure they know basic first aid and survival skills. Talk about what to do if a separation or trauma occurs.

～ 60 ～

He's Broken Curfew Again

"He's late again. It's after midnight! He knows he's supposed to be home by eleven." Ann Ryan was pacing as her husband, Sam, watched the news on television.

"Randy is seventeen," he reminded her. "He's trying his wings."

Ann frowned. "He's still our son, he's still living at home, and we're still responsible for him. We set this curfew for a good reason."

Sam turned off the television and faced his wife. "Ann, I know you worry about Randy. I'm concerned about him, too. But we've argued with him so much about this curfew business, that I'm afraid we aren't going to accomplish anything positive at all if we stay up and confront him again tonight."

"But how do we know he's *safe?*" Ann asked. "He hasn't called, and as far as we know he could be lying on the road out there somewhere."

Sam nodded. "I understand that you're worried. We live in a crazy world. Randy knows we love him and that we worry about him."

Ann shook her head. "I'm not so sure he does realize we worry about him. As a matter of fact, after the last few weeks, he may even be doubting that we love him. We've done so much arguing."

Before Sam could answer, Randy opened the door and came in, looking surprised to see his parents standing in the living room.

Ann couldn't resist. "Randy, where have you been? You are more than an hour late—I've been worried sick!"

Randy's face clouded with anger. "Mom, I'm here, OK? It's no big deal."

Sam looked at him sternly. "It is a big deal, young man. Your mother and I are concerned about your health and well being."

Randy looked exasperated. "Why don't you just trust me? I don't know why you can't trust me."

Ann nodded. "Oh, Randy, of course we trust you. But the world does have an awful lot of bad people in it. We just want to make sure you're safe."

Randy started to walk upstairs. Sam reached out and put his hand on his arm.

"Son, we need to work this out. This is the third time this month that you've violated the curfew set for you."

Randy shrugged. "Just go ahead and ground me again. That's what you always do."

Sam nodded. "And I can see how effective it has been," he mused. "Let's sit down for a few minutes before you go to bed."

Randy reluctantly sat down with his parents in the living room. Sam began the conversation.

"Randy, why do you stay out later than the curfew your mother and I have set for you?"

"Eleven is too early for a weekend," Randy answered quickly. I barely get off work and get over to my friend's house, when it's time to come home. I want some time for myself."

"But Randy," Ann objected, "you don't even call me to let me know you're safe!"

"Mom, I can't search out a phone every time I'm going to be a few minutes late. Besides, my friends will think I'm a momma's boy or something!"

Sam thought for a moment. "Randy, do you usually go to the same friend's house every weekend?"

Randy shook his head. "No. But I usually end up at one of three of my friends' places."

Sam nodded. "We might be willing to extend your curfew by an hour on the weekends if we knew for sure that you were in a safe place. Would you be willing to give us the phone numbers of those friends? We wouldn't call unless you were out past the extended curfew or we had reason to believe you might be in danger."

Randy hesitated. "But what if we're out cruising or going to a movie or something?"

"Son, the bottom line is that your mother and I need to know you are in a safe place. It's up to you to communicate to us where you are and how safe it is. We won't argue much about the length of time you are gone as long as you are careful to tell us where you are and that it's safe."

Randy thought for a moment. It would sure make life easier if he wasn't always arguing with his parents.

"OK," he agreed. "I'll give you the phone numbers, and I'll figure out how to let you and Mom know I'm all right and in a safe place when I'm out. But you can't embarrass me by calling me at my friend's house unless it's really drastic."

"Sure," both parents chimed in unison.

Randy yawned. "Let's start tomorrow night," he suggested. "I'm going to a party at Cliff's. I'll leave the number by the phone. And, I'll see you at midnight."

His parents nodded.

As Randy walked up the stairs, he paused and looked down at them.

"I'm really not a bad kid," he reminded them. "You can trust me."

Recognize the Strength

Exercising independent judgment is a skill every teenager needs to develop, and Randy is trying to do that. Although most parents worry that their teens will make drastic mistakes, most kids will respond positively to a calm and reasonable approach.

Focus on Accountability

Teens like Randy, who have received a solid foundation of love and concern from their parents, will benefit by recognizing that a big part of their responsibility lies in communicating with those who love them most. As in any compromise, both parties need to be aware of how the actions of each are affecting the other. The curfew stands for a very good reason. If the teenager understands the reason, the chances are very good there can be an understanding between child and parent that promotes a positive relationship. By discussing accountability, both the teen and the parents can determine the best course of action to reach the goal.

～ 61 ～

Don't Be Such a Pushover

"Sandy, where is your new bicycle?" Nancy Smith looked at her eleven-year-old daughter, knowing the answer to her question already.

"Well, I let Connie borrow it," Sandy replied. "She wanted to go over to her friend's house."

Nancy tried not to show her frustration. "Sandy, you let your sister help herself to anything of yours she wants. You do have a right to keep a few things for yourself, you know."

Sandy shrugged. "I know. I don't really care if Connie uses my stuff, though."

Nancy walked into the kitchen where her husband was putting the finishing touches on dinner. "What are we going to do about Sandy?" she asked him. "She lets her sister walk all over her!"

Robert Smith turned in surprise. "Sandy's our sweetheart. Don't you want her to be kind and unselfish?"

Nancy shook her head. "It's not that. She's too unselfish. She's becoming a pushover. I don't want people to walk all over her. She needs to learn to stand up for herself, especially when it comes to her strong-willed sister."

Robert smiled. "Connie is a pretty domineering sibling, as older sisters go," he admitted. "But Sandy doesn't really seem to be suffering. She adores Connie and tries hard to be like her."

Nancy frowned. "Well, we're pretty sure that Connie will be able to stand up for herself in the real world. She's got a strong will and outgoing personality. But what if Sandy lets everyone take advantage of her the way Connie does? Shouldn't we try to make sure Connie doesn't overshadow her sister?"

It was Robert's turn to shake his head. "I really don't think Sandy is a weak person. I think her relationship with Connie offers a measure of security."

Nancy looked doubtful, but further conversation was interrupted by thirteen-year-old Connie bursting through the back door.

"Mom! Dad! I'm starving! When do we eat?"

Nancy smiled in spite of herself. Connie had a way of bringing almost electric energy into a room.

"Five minutes," she told her. "Go get your sister and come sit at the table."

A few minutes later, as the four of them sat around the dinner table, Nancy decided to bring up the issue of Connie's taking unfair advantage of her sister.

"Sandy," she said, "did you get your bicycle back from your sister?"

Sandy looked at Connie, and hesitated. "Well, kinda."

Robert frowned. "What do you mean?"

Sandy looked uncomfortable. "Well, Connie said she traded my bike to Sylvia for a week in exchange for getting tutored in math by Sylvia's brother."

Connie nodded. "Dad, he's really good, and I need to get a better grade so I can go to the Science Center field trip."

Nancy interrupted. "Connie, that's inexcusable! Your sister won't have her own bicycle for a week because of your selfish actions. Didn't you even think about asking Sandy before you did it?"

Connie shrugged. "Mom, Sandy said I could use her bike for as long as I want. Besides, I told her I would let her use something of mine as a trade."

Sandy nodded. "It's OK, Mom. We made a deal. And Connie promised she'd get my bike back for me after the week is over."

Nancy was exasperated. "Sandy, for heaven's sake. Don't you ever get tired of being the one who gives in? Why do you let your sister run your life?"

Both Connie and Sandy looked surprised. Connie spoke first.

"I don't run her life," she objected. "She likes it when I take charge."

Sandy nodded. "I don't let Connie run *everything*," she said. "But if I didn't let her be in charge of *almost* everything, we'd fight all the time, and I hate to argue."

Nancy exchanged glances with her husband. She knew Sandy inherited her peacemaking tendencies from her father. And she certainly couldn't disagree with the results of Sandy's efforts. Overall, the sisters argued much less than other families she knew.

"Well," Nancy conceded, "the two of you may have worked this out between you, but I do want you both to be sure things don't go too far when it comes to taking advantage of each other. I don't want to nag, but I do want to reserve the right to speak up whenever I think things are going too far."

"Sure, Mom," Connie agreed. "No problem."

Sandy nodded and smiled. "OK. I promise I won't let Connie always have her way. But there *is* one thing I really like about Connie being in charge."

Nancy turned to her. "What's that?"

Sandy grinned. "Well, whenever we get in trouble, I can honestly say it was Connie's idea. I'm just the one who gives her support. I kinda like that."

Robert smiled at his wife. "I *told* you Sandy liked the security," he reminded her.

Nancy sighed. "OK, OK. I give up. Let's get these dishes cleaned up and you girls can go back to whatever it is you're doing."

Connie looked at her mom and grinned. "Boy, Mom, you're a pushover!"

Recognize the Strength

The role of peacemaker in a family can often be misunderstood and interpreted as simply being too easily led. If you have a child like Sandy, you can point out the advantage of being able to compromise and negotiate with a domineering sibling or friend. Sandy recognized how she could avoid a great many arguments with her sister, and she has learned how to turn her subordinate position into one of security.

Focus on Accountability

Both the domineering and the submissive sibling need to be reminded of the effect their actions have on each other. Although a parent can allow a great deal of flexibility when it comes to the negotiations between the siblings, it's important to keep everyone aware of what's going on. Make sure *everyone* is stretching at least a little to accommodate the other person.

~ 62 ~

Do I Have to Draw You a Picture?

"Marie Elizabeth Martin, come here this instant!" Esther Martin was very frustrated, and her ten-year-old daughter knew this was the last call. She dropped her paintbrushes onto the newspaper beneath her art project and raced into the dining room, where her mother stood with hands on hips.

"Marie, you have not done one single thing I told you to do this morning." Marie looked guilty. "You have three simple chores to do—make your bed, take your clothes hamper to the laundry room, and feed the cat. How many times do I have to tell you this?"

"I'm sorry, Mama." Marie offered her apology with a smile. "I forgot. But wait till you see what I drew! I got a great idea at the last minute, and now I just know I'll have the best art project ever!"

"Marie, this is the same routine you are supposed to do every day." Her mother struggled to remain angry while she looked at Marie's shining face. She could feel herself relenting already.

"Marie," she said in a gentler tone. "I'm very glad your art project is working out so well. But sweetheart, you know there's work to be done. We even wrote out a list for you and posted it on the refrigerator. You agreed to do those chores in exchange for that new set of paints and brushes."

Marie nodded her head. "I know, Mama. Honestly, I just forget! Now will you come see my project?"

Esther followed her enthusiastic daughter into the bedroom and had to admit the painting was extraordinary. *Why couldn't Marie be as good at remembering her chores as she was at remembering how to mix colors and create shadows?* she thought. And then it occurred to her.

"Marie, what if you drew pictures for the chores you're supposed to do? I'll put that drawing on the refrigerator instead of our written list. Then you may remember better, and we'll all get to see your artwork every day."

Marie thought the idea sounded good. Esther suggested she do the three chores that were waiting for her right now, and as she was working, she could be thinking about the pictures she would draw to represent them. Marie agreed, and started off.

The next day, Marie's dad noticed a wild new drawing on the refrigerator. "What's this?" he asked Esther.

She smiled. "That's a picture of the chores Marie does every day."

He shook his head. "How can you tell what's what? It looks pretty abstract to me."

Esther grinned. "Well, it doesn't matter if you understand it. The point is, Marie can tell and she's in there making her bed as we speak."

Dad shrugged his shoulders and smiled again. "Well, you've certainly mastered the 'art' of dealing with our daughter!" he said.

Recognize the Strength

Tapping into the natural artistic ability your child displays is a great way to direct attention toward the task that needs to be accomplished. In Marie's case, drawing pictures of the chores she had to do seemed to be a successful way of encouraging her to remember and complete the jobs.

Focus on Accountability

Marie wasn't deliberately trying to escape her chores, she was just preoccupied with her artistic projects. Chores just weren't what she was naturally inclined toward thinking about. Most of the time her head was full of wonderful pictures of what she would create next. When we can work *with* children to use their natural bents—in this case artistic ability—we will see a higher degree of success in getting them to accomplish what we want them to do. They learn and remember better because they are using an approach that makes sense to the design of their minds.

~ 63 ~

You Call That a Thinking Noise?

The sounds coming from the back seat were almost deafening. Betsy Griffith was ready to tear her hair out. "Matthew! Miranda! Keep your voices down!" she shouted. Her six-year-old fraternal twins shrieked with surprise at their mother's tone. Their screams were the last straw. Betsy pulled the car into the next available parking lot and turned around to confront both of them.

"I've had it!" she said sternly. "I want both of you to be quiet! *And I mean it!* I can't even hear myself think!"

Miranda looked at her mother. "But Mommy, Matthew has to talk to me. If he doesn't talk, I don't know what he's thinking about."

Betsy shook her head. "Miranda, you guys weren't talking—you were just making lots of noise."

Matthew was humming and tapping his foot against the side of the car.

"Matthew? Are you listening?" He nodded. Betsy was getting exasperated. "Will you just not make any noise for at least a minute?"

Matthew looked puzzled. "What noise, Mommy?"

"Matthew, you are constantly making noise. If it's not humming, it's tapping, or rapping, or popping. I don't know how in the world you can even think."

Miranda spoke up for her brother. "Mommy, that's how Matthew thinks. He makes noise *to* think."

Betsy paused. Strange as it seemed, it made sense. Matthew had always been the more shy of the two children. But even though he didn't do a lot of talking, he did make most of the noise. Even while he was doing his homework he was humming under his breath or saying the words he was reading aloud. Betsy sighed. If only she didn't need the quiet to concentrate!

"OK you two," she said. "Let's make a deal. I know you understand the difference between your 'inside' voice and your 'outside' voice. What do you think about our having an 'inside' noise and an 'outside' noise? When we're in the car, I need you to keep all the noises you make as soft as you possibly can. That will help me be a safer driver. When you're outside, you can make all the noise you want. What do you think? Do we have a deal?"

Two heads nodded in unison.

As she drove away, Betsy heard whispering in the back seat.

"Good job, you two. That's a good level for inside noise."

"What did you say, Mommy? We didn't hear you!"

"Never mind—I was just thinking out loud!" their mom said cheerfully.

Recognize the Strength

"Thinking noise" is literally the way some children engage their mental powers. Verbal sound may be an indication of linguistic intelligence, which is the ability to use words wisely when expressing oneself. If it is combined with a rhythm or beat, it can also be an indication of musical intelligence.

Focus on Accountability

Helping children like Matthew and Miranda learn how much thinking noise is appropriate in various situations—like inside and outside—will help them become more sensitive to other people's needs. Matthew is not unique. Many people need varying levels of noise to think. Some like a radio playing all the time. Some can learn almost anything if it's set to music. What may work for one person may be very distracting to someone else. When two people with very different learning needs are sharing the same thinking space, it becomes necessary for them to talk through the options that attempt to accommodate both sets of needs.

~ 64 ~

I Can Hear Music

"He's too much of a daydreamer. You've got to crack down on him or he'll never get anything done. All he wants to do is play that silly guitar!"

Sharon Wiley had heard her mother's lecture on many occasions. This time she was determined not to give in.

"Mom," she explained patiently, "Darren has a real gift for music. I want to help him succeed by working *with* him instead of *against* him."

Her mother held up Darren's report card. "Well, someone's going to have to do some work, because these grades are very poor. Darren's in ninth-grade—his marks are going on his permanent record now."

Sharon nodded, but spoke softly. "Darren is thinking about his future in terms of a musical career. If I make him sacrifice his practice time and force him to sit at his desk and do homework, I don't think he'll concentrate on his homework anyway. I don't think he sees the connection between academics and music."

Her mother looked concerned. "Are you saying you're not going to insist he get his homework done if it conflicts with his practice schedule?"

Sharon shook her head. "No, mother, I'm not saying that. I'd just like to try an experiment that might help Darren in both areas."

At that moment, a tall, lanky teenager walked into the kitchen carrying a well-worn guitar case. The two women in his life who loved him most, greeted him warmly.

"Darren," his mother said, "I have an idea I'd like to run past you."

He shrugged and sat down, "OK."

Sharon continued. "Darren, we're disappointed in your grades. I'm sure you are, too. Your grandmother and I want very much to see you succeed, and I believe *you* want to do well in school."

"But school's more than just music, young man," interrupted his grandmother. "You've got to hit the books."

Darren groaned. "Grandma, I'm trying. Honest, I am. But school is really boring and I don't understand a lot of the stuff we do in math and science. I just want to be a musician."

Before his grandmother could reply, Sharon spoke up. "OK, Darren, I understand that, and I want to be supportive of your desire for a musical career. But I'd like you to try something that may work both for improving your music and improving your grades."

Darren looked interested.

"Suppose you practice your music while you are doing your homework?" Sharon asked. "I know you can't write reports and lessons and play the guitar at the same time, but what if you form a small study group of friends. They could talk you through some of the assignments while you play background music? Then, when you put your guitar down to write, I'm sure it will all be in your head, and it won't take you long to finish your assignments."

Darren's grandmother was shaking her head. "It won't work. The boy can't concentrate with music playing," she objected.

Darren looked at her. "Grandma, I can only concentrate when there *is* music. I think it's a good idea. At least it's worth a try."

Sharon reached out and put her arm around him. "Darren, I know there is no magical formula, but I am willing to try some unconventional methods if they might help you get through school successfully. You're going to be a great musician—I want you to be a well-educated one."

Darren smiled. "Thanks for your confidence, Mom. I'll call David and Tiffany. I think they'd come over and help me."

His grandmother was still shaking her head. "I don't see how you young people will accomplish anything if you sing and play your way through school."

Darren hugged her. "Grandma, if I get a *B* in science, would it matter whether I sang my way through the test or wrote the answers while I sat quietly?"

She frowned. "Well, it would to me, of course. But I'd sure be happy to see that grade on your report card."

Darren stood up. "Then I'll see what I can do. See you guys— whoops—gals later."

As he left the room, Sharon looked at her mom. "Well," she asked, "do you think it has a chance of working?"

Her mother smiled. "Oh, I suppose it has a chance. After all, Darren is a very smart boy. I only wish he would get more settled and realize there's more to life than music."

"Hey Grandma!" Darren poked his head back through the kitchen. "I wrote a new song for you today. Do you want to hear it?"

Sharon watched her mother's face light up. "Go ahead, Mother. I'll make sure he gets his homework done later."

"Well, the boy does have a gift," her mother admitted as she quickly followed Darren into the living room.

Recognize the Strength

Darren is displaying the gift of musical intelligence. If your child also has such a gift, try to find a way to help him or her use that musical ability to accomplish other necessary tasks in life—such as studying. By utilizing musical ability, and combining it with academics and other tasks, kids like Darren can become more successful, because they are working with their strengths and not against them.

Focus on Accountability

The report card is a tangible way for schools to inform parents about academic progress. Children like Darren need to remember that there will come a day of accountability, and it is at report card time. They need to understand that no one is trying to discourage their talent, but that their parents are trying to find a way to help them combine gifts to assure academic progress. Ultimately gifted children must take responsibility for their course grades and learn how to work with their own learning strengths to earn good grades.

～ 65 ～

You're Old Enough to Know Left from Right

Dawn tromped through the back door and threw her wallet on the kitchen counter. She grasped the top of her head with both hands and in a muffled yell announced "I can't believe I flunked my driving test!"

Her mom put down a half peeled apple and paring knife, wiped her hands on the dish towel and grabbed a couple of cans of diet pop out of the refrigerator. "Do you have any idea why?" she asked, handing one can to Dawn.

"Because I'm so stupid!" Dawn said sternly.

"Honey, you're not stupid. You are upset, but you're not stupid." Her mom pulled a chair away from the table motioning her irate daughter to sit down. She seated herself on the other side of the table, watching her daughter pace back and forth.

"I'm so stupid," she complained again. "Do you know why I flunked? I can't believe it!" Finally starting to unwind, she sat down in the chair to begin retelling the story, exactly as it happened, from the very beginning.

"You know I only missed one question on the written test last week, right?" she reminded her mom.

"Yes honey, you were so excited to score 99 percent," Mrs. Weber said. "Just a reminder, you thought you were pretty smart then."

"Well, I did know the drivers manual inside out and backwards. Anyway, it was 2:10 P.M. when they called my name. I filled out a couple short forms and then a mean-looking uniformed lady said to show her the car I would be using for the driving test. She asked me to start the car and demonstrate that all the lights worked. She checked every one! I thought it was pretty stupid, but I did it anyway," Dawn explained.

Mrs. Weber was sipping her soda, thinking *Yes, this is my Dawn. She doesn't ever skip a detail when telling a story.*

"I don't think this lady has cracked a smile in a month," she continued. "In fact, I bet it's been a year. Anyway, I was pretty nervous but we started out on Cooper Road and about two-and-a-half feet from the corner of Cooper Road and Riverside Road, she told me to turn right. Guess what happened next?"

"Let's see, you signaled and turned right?" Mrs. Weber asked, assuming she was wrong, but hoping she was right.

"No, I'm too stupid! I got flustered about which way was right and which way was left and I turned LEFT! And, I forgot to signal! That's kindergarten stuff, I'm so stupid!" she blamed herself again, as the tears filled her eyes.

"Sweetheart, you are not stupid. I wish you'd quit saying that. You and I both know that you're an A student with a 3.8 grade point average. You've been accepted at the university and you have one scholarship already. You are not stupid. You've never been real fast at determining left and right, but usually with three or four seconds to think, you can do fine. This lady just wanted you to do it more quickly. So, what happened next?" she asked, knowing there was more to the story.

"Well, I did okay on the next couple things. I had to back around a corner, which I did just fine. The parallel parking was a piece of cake. I nailed it on my first try," Dawn said proudly.

"See, I told you," her mom added quickly for reassurance. "You're not stupid. It takes great visual-spatial intelligence and some logic and reasoning to parallel park. Many adults who have been driving for years can't do it very well."

"Yeah, like Mrs. Martin at church last Sunday. It took her three times," Dawn said, with some humor back in her voice.

"Is that all?" her mom asked, knowing the apples in the sink were turning brown.

"No. She must have decided the left-right thing was my weak spot so she did it again. Just before we got to the corner of Jefferson

Street and Peck Avenue, she asked me to turn left. Mom, I just went brain dead. I ended up signaling left and turning right. It's just not fair, we were so close to the corner I just didn't have time to figure it out. If she could just point which direction to turn I could do it," Dawn moaned. "Do you think I could ask them to point next time?"

"You could ask your driver-ed teacher, Mrs. Anderson. She might know. But I have an idea," Mrs. Weber suggested.

"What? What can I possibly do? She flunked me because I don't know which direction to turn! I still can't believe I flunked! I'm going to be laughed out of the school tomorrow." Dawn was sinking into despair again.

"Here's my idea," Mrs. Weber said with a gleam in her eye. "We'll make another appointment for a test next Tuesday morning. Then on Monday night, we'll polish your fingernails. Then, using another color, on your left thumb we'll brush on a big *L*, and on your right thumb we'll brush on a big *R*. They can't tell you not to do that. With both hands on the steering wheel anyway, you'll just have to glance down at your thumbnails and you'll know which way to turn."

"Mom, you're incredible! Why didn't we think of this sooner? Maybe I'll do five *L's* and five *R's*. This is wonderful!" Dawn smiled as she gave her mom a big hug.

The following Tuesday as she headed out the door with her Dad to try again, her mom yelled, "Good luck this time!"

Dawn turned and smiled and gave her mom an *R* thumbs up.

Recognize the Strength

Dawn had already demonstrated her mental skills and learning ability by scoring 99 percent on the written driving test, backed up by acceptance at the university with a scholarship. She is an intelligent, young lady, with a great future. Her mother was wise to look beyond the emotional despair of the moment to remind Dawn she had many ways to show how smart she was, including her visual-spatial skills, and her logical-mathematical abilities.

Focus on Accountability

Dawn was certainly motivated to pass this test and do her best. Because she had a good relationship with her mom, they could talk through the problem until they discovered a workable solution.

If Dawn wanted to get her driver's license, she had to find a way to overcome her nervousness about telling left from right. Painting a code on her fingernails was simply a safety net for helping her remember what to do under stress. Encouraging her to use creative solutions will help her cope with similar situations as she grows into adulthood.

~ 66 ~

You Have a Vivid Imagination

Katie came running home from school in the mid-October sun. As she burst into the house, she yelled, "Mommy, can I play in the leaves?"

Mrs. Perry was in the kitchen preparing dinner. "Sure," she answered, "but don't you want a snack first?"

"OK. Are there any apples left? I'd like an apple, please," Katie said.

Katie ate her apple quickly and was out the door in a flash. Her mom was amazed at how hard Katie worked raking leaves. First, she raked a small pile together, and then she ran around, dancing and prancing, waving her arms gracefully as if she had on ballet slippers instead of tennis shoes.

Mrs. Perry opened the kitchen window and called, "Are you dancing?"

"Yes!" Katie yelled. "I'm doing the Nutcracker and my prince has come!" Suddenly Katie lay down in the leaves and began flapping her arms and legs wildly.

Mrs. Perry watched for a while longer and then called, "Now what are you doing? Are you being a snow angel in the leaves?"

"No," Katie responded. She was back on her feet. "I already did that. I'm pretending it's raining." She was reaching into the pile, throwing handfuls of leaves up into the air, letting them swirl down on her head. "It's raining, it's pouring, the monkey is snoring!" she sang.

Mrs. Perry watched as Katie moved from one imaginative story to the next. She seemed to flit like a bee, landing on one idea momentarily and then moving on to the next one. Katie began raking wildly, taking leaves from every corner of the yard, and even some from the neighbor's yard, making a gigantic pile. Several minutes went by and Mrs. Perry looked out the window again. She saw a neat mountain of leaves but no Katie.

Slipping on her shoes and a sweater, she walked outside, glancing around. Katie was nowhere to be found. *She must be somewhere,* Mrs. Perry thought, so she called out "Katie, where are you?" No answer. Hmmm. This is unlike Katie, so she called out a little louder, "Katie, where are you?" As she circled the house, feeling uneasy, she saw the leaf pile wiggle. *OK,* she thought, *I should have known.*

"Katie, where are you?" she sang a little louder. The leaf pile wiggled again.

"Katie Perry. Katie Perry. This is mission control. Please advise Houston of your location, over," Mrs. Perry said in a nasal voice, as if speaking though a fuzzy microphone.

"Houston, this is Katie. You find me," a muffled voice said from the shifting pile of leaves.

Mrs. Perry smiled and thought, *Katie is so creative and has such a vivid imagination. I wish she could develop some of her ideas in a more thorough way. Her mind can wander the world over without ever leaving the neighborhood.*

"Mission Control to Katie Perry. Give me a hint, I can't see you," Mrs. Perry teased as she moved closer to the leaf pile.

"I'm right here, Mommy!" Katie yelled, exploding out of the pile. She was laughing so hard she flopped down in the leaves. "Mommy, this is a space ship, just like the one I want to fly some day."

"Honey, you are so creative, you can be anything you want to be when you grow up," Mrs. Perry said, sitting down in the leaf pile and giving her daughter a hug. She knew if Katie ever *were* to become an astronaut, Mission Control would have to work out a lot of the details for her!

"Katie," she said with a sparkle in her eye, "If you are ever part of the space program, I think you'll be designing spaceships for the astronauts to fly."

"Yahoo!" yelled Katie, and she pawed the ground as if she were a horse. "But first I'm gonna ride off into the sunset on my horse, Trigger." Katie laughed as she galloped around the yard.

Mrs. Perry laughed as Katie neighed and bucked her way back across the lawn.

"I'll be a cowboy astronaut!" she exclaimed.

I don't put anything past you, Mrs. Perry thought.

Recognize the Strength

For a child like Katie with an imaginative, global mind, new thoughts and ideas may come and go in a whirl. If you have a child like Katie, foster this creativity. Your child may become a great artist, inventor, designer, engineer, or creator of some kind. The genius of these creative kids has yet to be matured and cultured. How wonderful it is that the seed is already planted there and just needs time to grow and be nurtured.

Focus on Accountability

For a creative mind, jumping around through a myriad of ideas is an easy task. The ability to come up with creative ideas and solutions will always be a strength for this child. However, when a project is started and not finished, or when school work goes undone because the child's creative energy is flowing elsewhere, then you, as a parent, must step in. Helping the child follow through from beginning to end may require some added time and monitoring on your part. A frequent check of progress or talking him through a procedure or project may prove helpful. Ask your child what motivation it would take to get him or her to accomplish the goal. It's important to remember that for some kids, an occasion like playing in the leaves is reward enough. Parents and kids alike just need to cherish these creative moments. Not everything related to raising kids has to be a challenge. Not everything has to be a battle. Sometimes we just need to stop and smell the roses, enjoy the moment, and enjoy our kids.

～ 67 ～

I Can't Do Math

"I don't get it!" said Benjamin.

"What don't you get?" questioned Mr. Talley.

"I don't get math," Benjamin repeated.

Benjamin was a fifth-grader at Lakeside Elementary. He was a great student with a sense of humor and a big heart. Math, however, wasn't easy for him, and fractions were becoming a real frustration.

"Ben, would it help if for a while we didn't worry about the terminology for fractions—you know 'numerator' and 'denominator'—and which one was the top number and which one was the bottom number?" Mr. Talley asked casually.

"Maybe," Benjamin said. "If I just had a way to remember them without all the definitions. It's all so confusing. Yeah, I think it would help."

"Ben, how about attacking these fractions from a different perspective? Tomorrow we're going to try something new to see if it helps, OK?" Ben wasn't the only student who was struggling. Mr. Talley had already decided to tackle fractions a different way.

The next day, as the students went out for recess, Mr. Talley announced, "We're going to eat pie when you come back inside. So get your appetites ready."

"Pie?" Benjamin said. "I thought we had math after recess?"

"We do!" Mr. Talley said smiling.

"Cool!" several students chimed in as they ran outside to play.

Mr. Talley put all the necessary materials for the lesson on the empty desks. He set the apple pie on the front table, and then sat down to enjoy a quick cup of coffee. As the students returned to the room, many looked puzzled.

"Today, we're going to eat fractions," said Mr. Talley. The class cheered. Mr. Talley held up the apple pie. "If you went out to a restaurant for apple pie with five of your friends, into how many pieces would you cut the pie?"

Benjamin's sense of humor kicked in. "Seven, I want two pieces." Everyone laughed.

"Six," said Danny, "assuming one piece per person."

"Correct," said Mr. Talley. "Your group consists of six people. It also represents the number of pieces the 'whole' is divided into. Each person would get one-sixth of the pie. Does everyone agree?"

The class gave a corporate nod. Benjamin sat up a little straighter. It was starting to click. He could see where Mr. Talley was headed. *I can do this,* he thought.

Mr. Talley continued. Using the overhead projector, he explained the problems using the pie as an illustration. The class seemed to relax as they realized that fractions were pretty simple if you used Mr. Talley's method instead of the textbook definitions. *This is so easy, why didn't we start it sooner?* Benjamin thought to himself.

Mr. Talley divided the students into small groups and handed out problems and pieces of a paper pie. "As soon as we've finished our problems, we'll eat the real pie. Don't worry, I have a couple more pies. There'll be enough for everyone."

As he passed Benjamin, he asked, "How's this working, Ben? Does it make sense now?"

Benjamin flashed him a big smile. "It sure does, Mr. Talley. I guess all those definitions and rows of problems in the book didn't mean anything to me. They were just numbers I couldn't decipher. I like it when we do real stuff like this."

As the students talked and laughed and asked for more problems to solve, Mr. Talley determined that his extra effort was worth all the extra time it had taken to prepare. *I want* all *of my students to both understand and enjoy fractions,* he thought.

"Mr. Talley?" Benjamin interrupted. "Can I make up some of my own problems tonight? This is fun and it doesn't seem like math."

"Sure can!" Mr. Talley told him. *I think I'll do M&Ms tomorrow,* he thought.

Recognize the Strength

Benjamin appears to be demonstrating a concrete way of thinking when it comes to the abstract math concept of fractions. In his concrete way of thinking, he is great at specific tasks and appreciates having an actual hands-on model to practice or replicate. With his literal way of thinking, having a real-life situation like the restaurant dilemma was a great way to put into practice the concept he was learning. He needed to experience fractions using his five senses, trying to understand them by using taste, touch and smell to help bring meaning to the problems. Benjamin just needed the "math manipulatives"—the pieces of paper pie and some friends—to make the fraction problems come alive.

Focus on Accountability

Math concepts and math calculations do not come easily to many students. For students like Benjamin, approaching math from a practical, everyday situation can be most helpful. Students then begin to see why learning about the concepts is important. Without getting bogged down in the terminology, Mr. Talley was able to make the problems practical and real. He helped all of his students understand and conquer their math fears by helping the students find solutions to real-life problems and then moving to more abstract ideas involving applications and solutions.

～ 68 ～

Stop Hitting Me

"Stop it!" Paul complained to his brother.

"Oh shut up," Jeremy said. "You're such a baby."

The boys were sitting on the floor, putting on their shoes. It was time to leave for school. Jeremy moved his right leg ever so slightly and kicked Paul in the knee.

"Stop it!" Paul yelled. "Stop kicking me!" he moaned louder, hoping his mom would hear the ruckus. "Leave me alone!" Paul said even louder as he finally got one shoe on.

Mrs. Hill entered the doorway. "Boys, you're going to be late for school. Why don't you have your shoes on yet?"

"Jeremy is kicking me," Paul announced. "He won't leave me alone."

"Boys, we go through this every morning," Laurie Hill said with frustration in her voice. "I know the utility room is small, but can't you just leave each other alone and put on your shoes?" She turned around. "I almost have your lunches ready."

Paul looked at Jeremy, who stuck out his tongue. "You brat," Jeremy teased. He grabbed his other shoe and swung wide, just enough to bash Paul on the arm. He quickly jerked the shoe back and slipped it on his foot.

Tears flooded Paul's cheeks as he screamed, "Leave me alone!"

Laurie returned with two sack lunches. "Now what's going on?" she asked, seeing Paul's tears.

"He hit me with his shoe," Paul whimpered, wiping his eyes.

She crossed her arms. "I just don't know what to do with you two. We go through this same old routine every morning. Can't each of you just keep your hands to yourself? Do I have to stand over you and watch every move?" She sighed deeply, shaking her head. She handed the boys their lunches, kissed them goodbye, and watched as they headed down the street to school. As she looked out the kitchen window, they were laughing and talking as they walked.

That evening after dinner, Laurie recounted the events of the morning to her husband. "They are seven and nine; you'd think they would have it figured out by now."

Scott Hill looked at his wife. "I think they know what gets you going."

"Why do you say that?" she said defensively. "It sounds like you're taking sides."

"They pick on each other and you give them all the attention they need. Ignore it. Don't make such a big deal out of it," Scott said. "I'll talk to them. But try to lighten up a little."

Laurie was a little bewildered. *Oh well,* she thought, *maybe it's worth a try. Maybe if I leave them alone, they'll leave each other alone.*

Recognize the Strength

The boys' constant bickering may appear to be a sibling power struggle. But, believe it or not, these boys are learning to lead, to debate, and to negotiate to a satisfactory conclusion. When children are constantly arguing and fighting it's hard to remember that this is a time for sharpening their thinking and reasoning skills. The problem-solving strategies they are practicing will be very useful in later life.

Focus on Accountability

The arguing and fighting of childhood is tolerated better by some parents than by others. Children find it hard to understand how their squabbling affects the feelings and emotions of those listening. Parents who have lower tolerance for childish quarreling could try having the children take turns doing chores, or put in them in different areas when they are getting ready to go out the door. Put some space between them so they can't reach each other with words or actions. Rearrange schedules or rearrange the major events where the most fighting occurs to help you maintain your patience. Just remember that as they learn to work through conflict, difficulty, and rivalry, they are learning important skills that will stand them in good stead throughout their lives.

∼ 69 ∼

Why Is He So Quiet?

"How was school today?" Mr. Myers asked his son. He had heard Brett coming, whistling all the way down the street as usual.

"OK," Brett said, taking off his shoes and going in the house. Apart from the whistling, Brett was so quiet. Carrying on a conversation with him was usually one-sided. Even when a complicated question was asked, the answer was always short, concise, and to the point.

Mr. Myers followed Brett into the kitchen and helped him get a snack. "Are you making some new friends at school?"

"Not really," Brett said. They had moved to the neighborhood just a few days before school started.

"Are you getting to know the kids in your class?" Mr. Myers continued to probe.

"Not really," Brett answered in his quiet, introverted way.

On Tuesday, Phil and Lori Myers attended "Back to School Night" at Chesterfield Elementary. They entered the school, not knowing any of the other parents who were busy talking and laughing. They sensed how difficult this must be for Brett. They found room ten and entered to find Mrs. Turner, Brett's fifth-grade teacher, waiting for them.

"Hello. It's nice to have you here. Which of my students is your child?" Mrs. Turner asked in a perky voice.

"Brett Myers is our son," Phil volunteered.

"Oh, Brett. He's a fine boy. You are new here in Chesterfield. Welcome to the community," Mrs. Turner said warmly.

After looking at examples of Brett's work and flipping through some textbooks, Mrs. Myers inquired, "Is Brett making friends?"

Mrs. Turner looked at the Myerses while collecting her thoughts.

"Brett appears to be a very cautious, quiet child. When I put him in small groups with other children, he always participates and works hard. At recess, he interacts with a few of the boys, but he seems content to spend time by himself. Actually, I've found it easier to communicate with him by writing notes. He and I exchange several messages a day."

Phil snapped his fingers. "That's it. Great idea. I'm going to put up a memo board at home. Maybe Brett will write when he doesn't feel like talking."

Mrs. Myers nodded. "Brett must carefully think through his decisions. He never jumps to conclusions about anything. He just takes his time with everything. Maybe writing out his thoughts can give him the time he needs to communicate them."

Mrs. Turner smiled, "You have a wonderful son. It's certainly worth the time we take to hear what he has to say."

Recognize the Strength

Children like Brett will display a great deal of "self smart." They know themselves. These children, although quiet on the outside, may be very busy on the inside, thinking, analyzing, and figuring things out. Never assume that quietness means lack of intelligence. Instead, explore some methods of discovering what it is they are thinking.

Focus on Accountability

Quiet thinkers will be a bit more challenging to get to know. Whether orally or in writing, try to ask more open-ended questions that don't just require a "Yes" or "No" answer. Ask their opinion on a topic. Ask for a reaction to a news event or the grade on a paper. Be specific when seeking information from them. Help them understand you really value what they are thinking—what is inside their heads—and that you appreciate their thoughts. It may take more time than it does with other children, but it will be a valuable experience for both of you to share.

～ 70 ～

Am I an Overachiever?

Jenny was sitting in the chair crying. "I can do it. I know I can do it."

Karen Ronstat, the senior class counselor, handed her a tissue. "Jenny, you are what we call an overachiever. You want to accomplish more than you have time or energy to get done. Does that make sense to you?"

Jenny shook her head as she wiped her eyes. "I don't think it's overachieving. I have set very high goals for myself and I know I can accomplish them. I just think Mrs. Samm is being unfair."

"I need to know what you mean by unfair," Miss Ronstat asked. "I was told your project was a week-and-a-half late."

"Well, yes, but I had an out-of-town game that all the cheerleaders went to and a Future Teachers of America meeting to organize, and the honor society was having a car wash I helped with, and my church youth group went on a retreat, and…"

"Wait a minute, Jenny," Miss Ronstat interrupted. "You are an honor student. Think about what you just said."

There was a pause while Jenny hesitated. Then she admitted, "Well, I do keep plenty busy, but I still don't think I'm over- whatever."

Miss Ronstat suggested they make a list of commitments Jenny had. After a couple minutes, the list had grown to fifteen major activities. And "academics" was just one of them. "This is your senior year, Jenny."

"I know, and I want to accomplish all I can before I graduate," Jenny said optimistically.

"Let's be realistic, Jenny. As much as you want to, it is not physically possible for you to maintain your grades and do all the activities on this list, unless you sacrifice something," Miss Ronstat said. "Let's get back to the Mrs. Samm issue."

"It's not fair, she gave me an *F* on my project," Jenny protested.

"Was it a week-and-a-half late?" Miss Ronstat inquired.

"Yes, but it was a great project. I worked really hard on it. I should have an *A*. I don't deserve an *F*."

"Did Mrs. Samm give you a specific deadline or due date?" Miss Ronstat said.

"Yes."

"What was it?"

"November 18."

"And when did you hand it in?" Miss Ronstat continued to dig a little deeper.

"November 30, but see I really needed the extra time over Thanksgiving weekend because I had all that stuff to do... cheerleading...honor society..." her voice trailed off. "Over..."

"Overachiever?" Miss Ronstat suggested.

"Yeah. I guess I am one of those. OK, I get the point. By the way, did you hear the announcement in the daily bulletin about helpers needed for the spring play. I think that sounds like great fun."

"I'm not sure you *do* get the point," Miss Ronstat sighed.

Recognize the Strength

Jenny has great enthusiasm for all of the projects she takes on as her responsibility. Her orientation towards high goals will help her accomplish more in life than the normal person, and she will be very diligent in all she chooses to undertake. She does, however, need some coaching about the commitment of time she is making. She needs to learn how to make commitments that will fit into her already busy schedule.

Focus on Accountability

Jenny was missing deadlines because she was overcommitted. Miss Ronstat was wise in helping her see she didn't have enough time to complete everything, unless she wanted to sacrifice her grades, or something else. The quality of Jenny's work on the late assignment wasn't the issue here. The issue was that she had missed the deadline. Jenny and other overachievers may need to plot out on a calendar the major activities they participate in and the amount of time necessary for each one. By so doing, they will quickly grasp the idea that they are overcommitting their lives. This process may help them know how to cut back. For a while, they will have to make a conscious decision to say no to most of the events and activities that come their way. But with time, they may learn to strike a balance. If they cannot learn to control their time, they may have to learn the hard way to accept the consequences that come with sacrificed quality and missed deadlines.

∼ 71 ∼

Who Left Their Clothes on the Floor?

"Mom! Have you seen my new red skirt?" Robin Lane rushed breathlessly through the kitchen where her mother and aunt were having coffee.

"I believe you left it on the floor last night," her mother replied calmly. Robin's expression was one of panic.

"Oh, no!" she cried. "I'm *ruined!* I need that skirt for the student body elections assembly!" She raced back out of the room.

Karen Murphy smiled as her fourteen-year-old daughter disappeared through the doorway. Karen's sister, Alice, looked surprised.

"Why is Robin so upset? What's the big deal about leaving her skirt on the floor? Is it ruined?"

Karen shook her head. "No. It's a new policy we put into effect last week. I got so tired of picking clothes up off the floor that I told Robin I would impound every item of clothing I picked up, and she wouldn't get them back for one week. She didn't think it would really matter, but she's suddenly discovering how many pieces of clothing she leaves lying on the floor. Her wardrobe is shrinking."

Alice laughed. "Boy, I really would have been in trouble if Mom had done that to *me!*"

"I know," agreed Karen. "You were always the messy one. It drove me crazy when we had to share a room!"

Karen stood and began to clear the table. Alice thought for a moment.

"Karen, Robin's a great kid. She's always been a little on the messy side, but she's so busy with a jillion activities, she can't keep up."

Karen nodded. "That's true," she admitted. "But Robin herself gets frustrated when she can't find things she needs. She even admitted she'd like to become more disciplined and organized."

"Uh oh," Alice said with a grin. "That was your golden opportunity!"

Karen nodded. "Robin and I have argued for years about the condition of her room. I've tried everything to get her to keep it clean. She prefers to live her life like a whirlwind, bouncing from one place to another, without bothering to pick up the pieces. None of her boundless energy has gone into keeping her room organized or uncluttered! I've just had enough when it comes to all the wrinkled clothes and dirty laundry. Robin needs to learn the value of wearing something more than once before it ends up in a heap."

"But how do you impound her clothes?" asked Alice.

"I give her all evening to pick things up, and then in the morning, right up to the time she leaves for school. After she's gone, I go into her room and scoop up all the clothes that aren't hanging up or in the laundry hamper. I have a box marked with the date a week from that day, and I put the clothing in and store it on my closet shelf. She can't have that box before the date marked on the outside."

Alice was shaking her head. "Wait—I thought this sounded like a good idea for me to use with Roger, but I'd have a terrible time keeping track of those dates and boxes *myself!*"

Her sister shrugged. "So don't worry about exact dates—just keep a weekly box and accumulate the clothes for seven days, then don't give them back until the same day the next week. Believe me, Robin has really started to pay attention to what she leaves lying around on the floor!"

At that moment, Robin came swooping into the kitchen again, having changed into comfortable jeans and sneakers. "Gotta go, Mom. Study group meets until six. See you later!" She started out the door, then quickly turned and came back."

"Wait! I think I left my shoes in the bathroom—I better put them in the closet. Mom, don't go in there yet—I've got some more work to do before I go to bed!"

As she darted past the door, Alice grinned at her sister. "Well, I have to hand it to you, Sis—she's paying attention!"

Karen looked pleased. "At least for awhile," she replied. "But I still haven't found a method to get my husband to pick up his clothes!"

Alice waved off the comment. "You'll think of something!"

Recognize the Strength

Often the messiest kids are the most creative and energetic. If you can get your children to admit the unkempt condition is becoming a problem, you will have a good opportunity for coming up with a method that will get them to direct some of that energy to the solution. The more creative you can be, the better your chances of success.

Focus on Accountability

Before you decide to make your child's messy room an issue, determine whether or not this is a battle that is worth winning. If your child truly feels frustrated with the clutter, go ahead and help design some strategies for coping successfully with the problem. With some children, you may need simply to insist that they leave nothing in their rooms that could turn into a living organism. Just close the door and keep the rules clear and simple. A solution like Karen's for Robin can help your child discover the potential benefits of having a clean room in the first place.

Why Can't You Just Do What You're Told?

Christina Smith was in trouble again. The restless first-grader squirmed in her chair as she waited to find out what sentence the principal would hand down for this mistake. Just then, her mother stepped into the office, walked over, and gave her a big hug. Mrs. Smith smoothed her daughter's hair and asked the inevitable question.

"Oh, Christina, what happened? We were so worried!"

Christina shrugged as Mr. Rogers, the assistant principal, opened his door and beckoned to them. Christina's teacher, Mrs. Fulton, was already sitting in the inner office; everyone else came in and sat down. Mr. Rogers looked very stern.

"Mrs. Smith… Christina… we have a real problem here. Christina has been missing from her classroom for almost an hour. We've all been searching for her and this has seriously disrupted our routine—again. Christina, Mrs. Fulton tells me she gave you permission to take a jacket to the lost and found, but you completely disappeared instead of returning to class."

Mrs. Fulton spoke up, not directing her comment to any person in particular. "It was a simple request. I made myself quite clear. The jacket was evidently left by one of the students who had been using our classroom while we were at recess. Since Christina has so much energy, I thought she would benefit from running a quick errand."

Christina looked at her teacher, hoping for a smile of reassurance. Finding none, she scooted a little closer to her mother. Mr. Rogers was opening a manila file folder on his desk.

"Mrs. Smith," he began. "This is yet another incident that shows a predictable pattern of inattention on the part of your daughter. She

225

seems incapable of following even the simplest of directions. I really believe it would be in Christina's best interest to have her tested for the possibility of an attention deficit disorder."

Mrs. Smith smiled politely, trying to pull her thoughts together. She wanted to maintain positive relationships with Christina's teacher and administrator, but she knew better than anyone that there had to be a logical explanation for her daughter's behavior. She tried to choose her words carefully.

"Mrs. Fulton, Christina loves you. I don't believe she would deliberately disobey you. I'd like to hear her reason for not returning to the classroom promptly." She turned to her daughter. "Christina, you had all of us very worried. You know better than to take off without telling anyone where you are going. What were you thinking about?"

Christina brightened and seemed eager to explain her reasoning. "Well, it's really cold today, and I knew that the kid who lost the jacket would need it right away. I just visited the other classrooms to see if it belonged to anyone."

Mrs. Fulton looked exasperated. "Christina, didn't you *listen* to me when I told you to take the jacket to the office and come right back?"

Christina nodded. "I just had a better idea," she said cheerfully.

Mrs. Smith smiled at Christina and gave her a quick squeeze. "Sweetie, I need you to wait for me right outside the office here. I'll be out in just a few minutes. Where will you be sitting while you wait for me?" Christina got up and pointed to one of the chairs outside the door. After she left the room, her mother looked at Mr. Rogers and Mrs. Fulton. "Christina doesn't think like many children—that's true. But I have to admit I admire her resourcefulness, and I truly appreciate her thoughtfulness in this particular situation. Are there some steps we can take before we decide this is simply an attention problem?"

Mrs. Fulton was smiling for the first time since the conference began. "Mrs. Smith, I believe you just demonstrated what Christina needs when it comes to directions. I need to be much more specific about where she is supposed to *end up*. I sometimes get so busy, I just don't stop to remember that she is a child whose mind will find many different ways to accomplish a goal. I'll certainly try to be very clear about the *outcomes* I want her to demonstrate."

Mrs. Smith looked relieved. "Mrs. Fulton, now I know why Christina loves you! Thanks so much for understanding. What can I do to help Christina focus on what you ask her to do?"

Mr. Rogers watched in admiration as both women called Christina back in and spent the next few minutes encouraging her to use her creative energies to meet some very specific goals. He couldn't help wishing every conference could end on such a positive note!

Recognize the Strength

Christina, like many children, has a knack for recognizing and meeting the needs of others. She has a sensitive and compassionate heart. She is also able to step back from the immediate, obvious situation and see the bigger picture. In the future, this will certainly be considered a great advantage when she uses creative thinking and problem solving.

Focus on Accountability

Because Christina's natural bent is to see the big picture, she may need help in focusing on the details. If the goal is to have Christina follow specific directions, she will need to know what the specifics *are*, and be able to recognize when she has achieved the outcome. After giving the directions initially, it may help to ask her to clarify what she will be doing, and give her a quick reminder of the result you are seeking.

～ 73 ～

I Can't Do an Outline

"Outlining is dumb," said Alan. "I didn't get it as a sixth-grader and I don't get it any better now as an eighth-grader."

"Dumb isn't a strong enough word," Derek added. "I could think of a whole *bunch* of words that describe it."

Mrs. Martin had droned on with her boring, dry explanation of outlining until the bell rang. Now Alan and Derek were headed down the hall, eager to escape Language Arts class. They were more than ready to enter room forty-two—the science classroom.

"We're going to outline chapter nine today," their teacher, Mr. Davidson said as the bell rang.

Moans and groans rose from everywhere in the room, silenced momentarily by the tardy bell. They could hardly believe their ears. Outlining in science!

"But," continued Mr. Davidson, "we're going to do it my way. And we'll start with chapter eight." His students quieted down. When Mr. Davidson said *my way,* they knew they were in for something unique.

"This has to be better than Martin's way," Derek whispered.

Mr. Davidson started his presentation by saying, "This is a review of chapter eight. What did we study last week in chapter eight?"

"Sharks," someone volunteered.

"Correct," said Mr. Davidson. He twisted around and wrote the word "sharks" in the center of the chalkboard. "Now tell me, what were some of the major categories of information we learned about sharks?"

"Mating and reproduction," suggested Tyson.

Everyone snickered. "Cute, Tyson," Mr. Davidson answered, and he wrote the category all the way to the left on the chart, drawing a line to attach the two categories. Mr. Davidson continued, "This is called 'webbing' or 'mapping.' You can continue adding branches under the major categories. Then you can branch off again and list more facts under each category. You can make these webs as simple or as complicated as you like, depending on how much you add to the original topic." As a class they added several more categories.

"This will make outlining a cinch," Alan whispered to Derek. "Too bad Mrs. Martin doesn't have this method figured out."

"Now that you see how it works," Mr. Davidson continued, "we're going to move into chapter nine. We will build a quick skeleton map or web just by skimming the chapter headings. To add more detail to the information in this chapter I've planned a couple of great experiments. Also, I want to show you a video and use a CD-ROM. We'll explore chapter nine in depth, webbing as we go."

Comments were coming from all around the room. "Cool," "Right on," "Awesome." As he strolled down the row of desks, Alan looked up.

"You just saved my life in Language Arts," Alan admitted.

"How?" Mr. Davidson inquired.

"Because Mrs. Martin makes us outline the old-fashioned way, by starting with the first paragraph. I just can't do it that way. This makes so much sense to my brain. Everything's coming back to me!"

"It's OK, Alan. I'm a grown man and I just learned this way of outlining. After all these years it finally makes sense to me, too. I decided you students didn't need to wait as long as I did to learn an easier method. Glad you like it. Now let me show you how to make Mrs. Martin happy, too."

Mr. Davidson showed the whole class how to quickly turn the completed web into a traditional outline. He used each section of the drawing as a heading or subheading for the formal outline. In less than five minutes, Alan had written an outline even Mrs. Martin would have been proud to accept.

"I didn't know I was this smart!" he exclaimed.

Recognize the Strength

Alan thinks in a global, big-picture way, and one of his strengths is the ability to back away from the details and logic to see the big picture. Once he sees the big picture, it's easier to focus on the details. The method of "webbing" or "mapping" is a great way to organize information in more than just an outline form.

Focus on Accountability

In Mrs. Martin's class, Alan and his classmates were being asked to produce a standard Roman numeral outline as a way to organize information in a logical and sequential format. Even though it did not make sense to Alan's mind, he was able to use a nontraditional method to reach a traditional goal.

～ 74 ～

Get Off That Telephone!

"Has Mike Murphy called me back yet?" Roger Turner looked at his wife expectantly.

"Emily's been on the phone for the past hour," Kathy Turner replied. "I don't think he could have gotten through."

Roger's expression quickly clouded into anger. "She has *got* to get off that telephone!" he said tensely. "There are other family members besides her that live here."

Kathy nodded. "Roger, we've been through this before. We just need to find the best way to share time on the telephone. Emily loves to talk to her friends on the phone. As a matter of fact, she loves to talk to *everyone* on the phone!"

Roger frowned. "Well, she's got to cut down her chatting in the evening. We can't afford to get a fourteen year old her own private line."

Emily dashed into the kitchen where her parents were standing. "Guess what? Jonathan's mother is going to let him have his own telephone for his birthday! That's so cool!"

"Emily," her father said sternly. "I've been expecting a call this evening, but you've been on the phone for more than an hour."

"Oh, it's OK, Dad. I didn't hear anyone beeping in on call waiting. I always listen and put my friends on hold if there's another call."

The telephone rang, and Roger started toward it.

"I'll get it!" cried Emily. "Please, let me get it!"

Kathy put her hand on her husband's arm.

"Let her get it, Honey. She's a great receptionist—really. She loves fielding calls."

Roger listened as his daughter answered the telephone.

"Turner residence, this is Emily. Oh, yes sir, he's here. May I say who's calling?" She turned to her dad.

"Dad, it's Mr. Murphy. Do you want to take the call in here or in your bedroom?"

Roger looked surprised. His wife nudged him. "See? I told you she's great with the telephone!"

After he completed his phone call, Roger found Emily in the family room. "Hey, Em, I need to talk to you."

She turned off the television and looked at him. He sat down beside her. "As you have noticed, I'm really frustrated with how much time you spend on the telephone. But I've got to admit, you do a nice job of fielding and screening calls for the rest of us. So let's make a deal."

"Shoot, Dad!"

"Well, you need to promise me you'll make sure your homework and chores are done before you talk to your friends on the telephone for more than two or three minutes. Then, if your work is done, you can talk up to thirty minutes at a time until bedtime. But you need to agree to continue listening for calls that come in while you are talking on the phone and hang up if any of those calls are for us."

Emily nodded eagerly. "No problem, Dad. I'll just be the one who answers the phone when I'm home and you won't even hear it ring!"

Roger smiled. "Emily, I don't think it usually has a *chance* to ring when you're home!"

Recognize the Strength

Although it may seem annoying, a child who talks incessantly on the telephone is showing a gift for conversation and public relations that can certainly be valuable as an adult. Helping your child learn to answer the phone in a prescribed manner can help cultivate a professional presence when talking to just about anyone.

Focus on Accountability

Even if you have a child who possesses a great deal of talent in talking to people on the telephone, it's important to help him or her keep priorities straight. If homework and chores are being completed, look for ways that your child's affinity for the telephone can be an asset to the family, such as becoming the resident receptionist or message taker. Talking through time limits and bottom-line accountability for other jobs that need to be done can also help your child assume responsibility.

~ 75 ~

I Hate Small Group Assignments

Not again, thought Keith to himself. *I hate group work.*

Mr. Thompson had just instructed the world history class to number off and get into six small groups for a new project. "You'll need to discuss the issue thoroughly and come to a group consensus. You'll also have specific responsibilities related to a group presentation that will be done in front of the class next week."

"Ugh," Keith moaned out loud. Not only did he hate small group discussions, but he especially disliked getting up in front of the class to do *any* oral report.

As the students began moving into their pre-numbered groups, Keith stood up to drag his chair to the back corner of the classroom where his group was meeting. *This is unfair and inhumane treatment,* he concluded. Reggie, the guy with the ego as big as the moon and an obnoxious attitude, was in his group. Not only was he stuck with Reggie, but Patty and Margaret were also in group number five. *They never stop talking,* he thought. *This is a nightmare in real life!*

During second lunch, Keith found Mr. Thompson in his office. With a friendly smile, Mr. Thompson invited him in. "Glad you could catch me right now," he said to Keith. "How can I be of service?"

Keith swallowed hard, looked at Mr. Thompson and said, "Is there any way I can do a different project?" He stumbled through a weak reason about not getting the newspaper delivered at his home.

Mr. Thompson sat very still, seeming to read Keith like a book. After a brief pause he leaned forward and looking at Keith, he said, "Keith, what's the real reason you want an alternative assignment?"

Keith stammered, "Mr. Thompson, Patty and Margaret just never stop talking. They drive me crazy. It's so distracting because part of the time it's not about the project. It's about guys or clothes or makeup or movies—just about anything but the project. And Reggie has such a big ego. He really is a jerk."

Mr. Thompson kept watching him, not saying a word. Maybe he knew this wasn't the real reason either. "Mr. Thompson," Keith paused, "I guess I really don't like small group activities because I feel like other students take credit for the work I do. I just like to do the work myself, so I know it's done right."

Mr. Thompson leaned back in his chair, clasping his hands behind his neck. "Keith, do you know why I occasionally assign group projects?"

"No," Keith responded, although he figured it was to irritate him and others like him.

Mr. Thompson explained, "It is to help students of differing opinions work through a problem to reach a solution." He also mentioned the benefits of the students who have trouble achieving academically, working with students of higher achievement. Working together would give them peers who could model good work and good study habits.

"That's why I believe they take advantage of me," Keith said. "My hard work gets them a better grade. It's not fair."

"There's another important reason," Mr. Thompson looked at Keith seriously. "Keith, you have the skills needed to get a management position in big business after college—or any other profession you choose to pursue. You are an intelligent young man with great potential. But I can tell you that many employers are looking for skills other than academic grades. They want workers and managers who can both demonstrate leadership skills and who can work cooperatively with a team."

Keith sighed and responded, "So you want me to just do the group thing, don't you?"

"Not just *do* it," Mr. Thompson said. "Keith, I'd like you to assume a leadership role. See if you can get everyone in your group to work together to communicate well and to produce a great final project that represents teamwork. Take this as a challenge, one that will help you be more prepared for your career. It's more than just an assignment in my world history class. It's a chance to prepare for the future."

"Mission Impossible—accepted," said Keith, saluting Mr. Thompson.

Recognize the Strength

Many people enjoy working individually on projects. However, families and societies need the contribution of each individual to make the whole team successful. Students like Keith may just need an occasional reminder that one of their greatest contributions can be their leadership in a group.

Focus on Accountability

Keith needed the challenge from Mr. Thompson to look beyond the assignment and even beyond the grade to the skills he would be practicing when working with his group. Leadership is a lifelong skill that takes practice and patience to develop. Keith and other students like him need to be good role models, both as leaders and as students. Small group work can be a challenge, but learning to be a team player will be a skill with lifelong value.

～ 76 ～

I Want the Most Expensive One

"Jordan, these tennis shoes are much too expensive." Tina Johnson had to look up to meet the eyes of her growing thirteen-year-old son. They had been in the shoe store for almost an hour while Jordan tried to decide on a new pair of shoes.

"Mom, I *have* to have these," he insisted. "I'd get laughed out of my class if I showed up in *those*." He pointed to the sturdy, modestly-priced shoes Tina had set aside. She shook her head.

"Jordan, I'm sorry, but I can't spend your entire wardrobe budget on one pair of shoes."

"Well, I'm not wearing *those*," he stated simply. "I'll just keep wearing what I've got."

Tina looked down at his feet and frowned at the frayed shoes. He didn't wear laces in them anymore, and the soles were coming apart on both shoes. It had been quite a battle when they bought these shoes, too, she recalled. Jordan had stood firm that he could *not* show up at school in anything less than the best shoes. In fact, lately he had turned up his nose at anything less than the top of the line when it came to clothing, bikes, and sports equipment.

"Let's discuss this with your father," Tina told him.

Jordan shrugged and they left the store.

After dinner, Jordan ducked out and went to the family room to watch TV. Tina cornered her husband, Matt, and told him what had happened with the shoes.

"Matt, how can we afford to keep him clothed? He's determined not to look 'uncool' at school, and yet he knows we're not rich enough to always get him the very best that's available."

Matt nodded and sighed. He worked hard, and he really wanted his family to have the best. It was time to put a new family policy into effect.

He walked into the family room. "Son, if you'll turn off the TV, we'll discuss getting those shoes you want."

Jordan eagerly hit the off button.

"Great, Dad, I knew you'd understand! I can't get those *lame* shoes that Mom wants me to buy."

Matt shook his head. "Your mother's right. We can't afford the most expensive shoes. But I am willing to make a deal with you so that you can buy the shoes anyway."

Jordan leaned forward. "Yeah? What is it?"

"Your mother and I will put as much money toward the shoes as we would have paid for the other, more reasonably-priced pair. If you can pay the difference, you can have the shoes."

Jordan looked disappointed. "Aw, Dad, how am I going to get that kind of money?"

"Good question, Jordan," Matt replied. "You have your allowance, of course, and I'm willing to give you a bit of a raise if you want to add a few more responsibilities around the house. I'll also help you get squared away with whatever you'll need to deliver papers or mow lawns and do yard work."

Jordan brightened. "Hey, I could get a new bike so I can get more work done!"

Matt nodded. "And I'll make the same deal with the bike as with the shoes. We'll pay the price of a modest but reliable bicycle, and you can pay the difference if you want a more expensive model."

Jordan frowned. "It's going to take me a while to earn the money. What will I do *now?*"

"Jordan, your friends will have to understand that you are *working* for what you want. In the end, they will respect you as much as we do for earning the privilege of buying the best."

Jordan sighed. "I guess I probably don't have another choice, huh?"

Matt smiled and said, "That's right, but I have a feeling you'll be making the *right* choice if you close this deal with me."

Jordan extended his hand. "All right!"

Matt shook hands with his son and gave the thumbs-up sign to his wife, who was standing in the doorway.

"I'll spring for dessert if you want to go get ice cream," Matt offered.

Jordan grinned. "Dad, do I have to pay the difference if I want extra scoops?"

Matt gave him a playful punch on the arm. "I think we can consider that one of your fringe benefits," he said.

Recognize the Strength

There's nothing wrong with wanting the best, and our children should be encouraged to use good taste in their selection of clothes and other items. Just as Jordan knew what he wanted, our children should be encouraged to recognize quality. They should also be encouraged to work for the privilege of having the best.

Focus on Accountability

Rather than simply giving our children everything they ask for, providing opportunities to let them earn the extra money themselves will help them appreciate what they purchase. If they want "the best" they must learn to earn the privilege of going "first class."

~ 77 ~

His Driving Lessons Are
Driving Me Crazy

"Isn't it your turn to give Tim his driving lesson?" Karen looked hopefully at her husband. Roger smiled.

"What's the matter, dear?" he teased. "Aren't your nerves as strong as you thought they were?" Karen gave him an exasperated look.

"Tim's a great kid—I love him very much. But all of a sudden, his traits that I've learned to appreciate the most are the hardest to deal with when he is behind the wheel of a car."

Roger looked puzzled. "What do you mean?" he asked her.

Karen sighed. "Well, Tim is just like you. He's analytic, systematic, and methodical."

"Yeah, well those seem like pretty good characteristics to me," Roger replied. "After all, they got me the job that got us that car that Tim's learning to drive!"

Karen hugged him.

"I don't doubt it at all," she said. "I'm just saying that a person can't afford to be quite so deliberate while driving in traffic. I tell Tim to watch out for the pedestrian, so he carefully watches the person crossing the street and forgets to look at the traffic signal ahead. I remind him to look both ways as he crosses the intersection, and he completely forgets to look in his rearview mirror at the car bearing down on him. He's really having trouble keeping track of everything at once and making quick responses in the heat of the moment."

Roger nodded. "Believe it or not, this sounds familiar. I had a hard time learning to drive."

Karen look surprised. "You? Roger, you're the best driver I know! How did you get over your tendency to over-analyze and pay attention to so many things at once?"

240

Roger looked thoughtful. "My dad told me that I should be doing one of three things at least every five seconds while the car was in motion: looking in my rearview mirror; looking left to right and back again; and scanning the road ahead for potential hazards. Somehow, quantifying it like that, my mind adjusted to the multiple tasks."

Karen nodded. "I think Tim would appreciate your sharing that tip. That gives me another idea, too. What if we encouraged him to play that *Race Car Ace* video game down at the pizza place? You know, the one that has you racing down the road and maneuvering around all kinds of sudden obstacles and problems? Maybe Tim could get more comfortable with split-second decisions if he could practice on a course that's not quite as threatening as real life."

Roger agreed. "In fact," he said, "I think maybe I'll have to go with him and supervise his instruction." He grinned. Just then the back door burst open and Tim walked in and plopped his school books on the table.

"Man," he said, "I can't believe my driver's ed instructor is so uptight. He doesn't let me drive nearly as often as the other kids in the class!"

Roger and Karen exchanged a knowing look. Then Roger reached over and gave his son a pat on the back.

"Hey, guy, we were thinking about having pizza tonight. You feel like going down to the pizza place on the corner?"

Tim brightened. "Sure! Can I drive?"

Roger tossed him the keys. "As a matter of fact, you *can*."

Recognize the Strength

Kids like Tim have a natural strength in the area of logic and analysis, so they may struggle with a task that calls for more intuition and instinct. A deliberate and methodical bent is the way their mind is designed to work, and may actually make them *better* drivers than others, once they learn the habit of monitoring the multiple tasks necessary while a car is in motion.

Focus on Accountability

Helping Tim quantify a seemingly overwhelming and nonspecific task is one of the best things his dad could do. Instead of making him feel like he's just not getting the hang of driving, Tim can now apply one of his greatest strengths to overcome the frustration of juggling so many things at once. Practicing with the video game can give Tim the confidence he needs to react quickly to real life driving challenges without risking his self esteem *or* the lives of others!

~ 78 ~

He's Cheating

Erica's eraser bounced on the floor and she bent to retrieve it. Behind her, Joe leaned forward at his desk. He just needed to see what she had for the answer to number twelve. He craned his neck ever so slightly. Two-hundred-seventy-five. How can that be? Joe recalculated once, twice, and then wrote two-hundred-seventy-five next to number twelve.

The bell rang and he slid his paper under several others as he left the room. "Erica, wait up." Joe sidestepped a couple of seventh graders to catch up. "How did you get two-hundred-seventy-five for problem twelve?" he asked.

She looked surprised. "How do you know that's what I got?"

"Because I looked over your shoulder," he admitted with a grin. "I didn't mean to, but you were bent over reaching for an eraser, and I just happened to see your paper."

"Well, I'd appreciate it if you would keep your eyes on your own paper," Erica said as casually as she could.

The following Friday was a repeat of the last. The class was working on another test in math but Erica had been moved to another seat. As they entered class Joe turned his back to the teacher and leaned over Todd's desk. "Can you help me if I get stuck on a problem?"

Todd was apprehensive. The request had caught him off guard. He was a little stunned.

Joe continued, "If I need help, I'll kick the back of your chair. Just slide your paper over to one side, lean over to scratch your leg, and I'll take a quick look at your paper, OK?"

The test had been predictable. Mr. Farley always used the same format, just changed a few formulas. Joe had kicked Todd's chair several times. Each time Todd had complied, scratching his leg while Joe craned his neck to pick out the answer. Erica watched from the back of the room, quickly decoding their secret. She couldn't believe it! Joe was cheating again, only using Todd this time. *How many other kids has he done this to?* she thought.

In the cafeteria, she found Todd with a couple of friends. "Todd, may I talk to you for a minute?" Todd slipped away from the table, grabbing a gulp of milk as he moved toward Erica. "May I ask you a question about the math test?" she asked nervously.

"Sure. It was a pretty predictable test, don't you think?" he responded, also a little nervous.

"Well, it's not really about the test. Last Friday, Joe cheated off my test and I didn't know it. But today I saw him cheating off your test, only you two had a system. He was kicking your chair. I'm ready to go to Mr. Farley and tell him what I saw. Do you want to come with me or should I tell on you, too?" Her voice was shaking by the time she finished. She hadn't planned to say all that, it just tumbled out after she started. She lowered her eyes to the floor. *Oh, brother! Now what have I gotten myself into?* she thought.

Todd stammered as he started, "I...I...Joe asked me to help him cheat just before the test started. I didn't know what to do. I don't want to be caught. I don't believe in cheating. May I go with you? We'll talk to Mr. Farley together."

Todd grabbed the remains of his lunch, pitched it in the garbage and the two students headed for Mr. Farley's room.

After the explanations were given and the ramifications discussed, Mr. Farley looked at both Erica and Todd. "You did the right thing, even though it was tough. I'm proud of both of you. I plan to submit both of your names for a Lion's Pride Award. We value honesty and hard work at Liberty Junior High, and you have certainly demonstrated those qualities today." He shook their hands as they left the room.

Erica looked at Todd. "Thanks for standing with me. I just hope I don't ever have to do this again."

"Me, too," said Todd. "I may have been duped the first time, but I'm glad I wasn't stupid enough to let it happen again. If it ever *does* happen again, I'll sure be prepared with a better answer."

"Besides, the solution he copied from me last week was wrong anyway, so it didn't help him a bit," Erica said, and they both laughed.

Recognize the Strength

Encouraging our children take a firm stand on moral issues, such as honesty, helps build integrity of character and sets levels of expectations that are worthy to work toward, both as a student and as a citizen. It was not easy for Erica to confront the wrongdoing of her classmate, but when she did, she chose to put her convictions ahead of momentary convenience.

Focus on Accountability

Honesty is a character trait we value at every age. It's easier to talk about it, but sometimes harder to put into practice when we're "under the gun." Erica was put to the test when she saw the cheating occurring. The easier path would have been to ignore Joe and Todd's game in math and protect herself from the wandering eyes of others. However, standing on the conviction that cheating was wrong gave both Erica and Todd a character-building experience that put inner strength in front of external convenience.

～ 79 ～

I Won't Eat It

"Amanda, finish eating your vegetables and I'll bring you your dessert." The little girl looked at her mother and shook her head firmly.

"I don't *like* vegetables," she said firmly.

Patricia Riley met her daughter's gaze.

Amanda shook her head again. "No, I don't want green beans," she insisted.

Patricia's husband smiled at his wife.

"I guess it's a woman's perogative to change her mind," he mused.

Patricia frowned.

"You're not helping," she told him. "If this child gets enough food in her to grow up, it will be a miracle."

Amanda was scooting her chair away from the table.

"I'm ready for cookies!" she proclaimed loudly. Her dad grinned.

"See, she *does* eat! Granted, it's not the right *food*, but at least she knows what she wants to eat," he said.

Patricia reached over and put the cookies out of reach.

"Well, there will be no cookies for Amanda until the green beans are eaten," she replied firmly.

Amanda seemed on the verge of pitching a fit, but she paused and looked thoughtful.

"When my beans are gone, I can have cookies?" she asked her mother. Patricia nodded, unaware that she was about to be out-smarted by her own words.

"Lucky! Here Lucky!" Amanda called the family dog, who eagerly responded. Before Patricia realized what was happening. Amanda had given Lucky the plate of green beans, and they disappeared in a flash.

"Amanda! *You* were supposed to eat those beans!" Amanda grinned.

"Mommy, you said as soon as the beans were *gone* I could have cookies," she replied.

Patricia felt her frustration level rise much too quickly. Her husband stepped forward to rescue the situation.

"Amanda, you know that's *not* what your mother meant. You cannot have the cookies at *all*, now."

Amanda was crying and protesting loudly.

"That's not fair! I want *cookies!*" Her father looked straight into her eyes.

"Amanda, you made a choice. Next time maybe you'll go ahead and eat the vegetables so you can have cookies for dessert."

Patricia knew her strong-willed daughter was about to dig her heels in, and the evening was going to go downhill fast if she didn't find a way to salvage it quickly. She sat down and put her arm around Amanda.

"Sweetheart, do you know *why* you need to eat vegetables?"

Amanda shook her head.

"Amanda, vegetables are a good source of vitamins and minerals that your body needs to grow strong and healthy."

"Can I get vitamins and minerals from cookies?" Amanda asked with a quizzical look.

"Let's read the label on the side of the cookies." Mrs. Riley pulled the package over to the table and they examined it together. "The label tells us that all we get from cookies are carbohydrates and fats. If we need to find some food that has vitamins and minerals on the label, where should we look?"

Amanda thought for a moment. Then a big smile lit up her face. "How about the orange juice carton in the refrigerator? Do we have some other cans of vegetables besides green beans in the pantry?" She quickly rounded up a few items from the kitchen that had nutrition labels. As Amanda and her parents scanned the information, they made some great comparisons.

"I know!" Amanda concluded. "If I can have orange juice, I can get more vitamins and minerals that from icky green beans! Then can I be done?"

"You know, Amanda, you're absolutely right," Mr. Riley said smiling.

"I guess we will all need to read the labels more carefully. Amanda, you've reminded Mommy of an important lesson. It's not really what we eat, but what the foods do for our bodies that is most important."

"Thanks for the good dinner, Mommy, 'specially the orange juice! Can I be 'cused?" Amanda kissed both her parents and skipped off to the play room.

"If only every problem were so easy to solve!" Mrs. Riley exclaimed.

Recognize the Strength

As a strong-willed child, Amanda made her own choice regarding the green beans for dinner. Her parents were able to use the strength of conviction, combined with some spontaneous problem solving, to allow Amanda to make some informed choices related to what she was going to eat.

Focus on Accountability

Amanda had a problem to solve. Actually, she had two problems to solve. She solved the green bean dilemma by feeding the beans to the dog. Because she is so strong-willed, her second problem was that she had gotten herself out on a limb and couldn't back down. Such situations between parent and a strong-willed child often become stand offs.

Her parents were wise to show her the food labeling, and let her draw her own conclusions. She was able to take some responsibility for good, nutritional choices, and she came up with a satisfactory alternative to the green bean issue.

Even at an early age, children can learn to compare nutrients and numbers on package labeling. This is a practical way to use math skills and a good way to teach wise eating choices. The bottom line for Amanda and her parents was to make sure she was getting the vitamins and minerals she needed to grow. Amanda very clearly came up with a choice she could live with, that was nutritionally sound and met her parent's criteria.

~ 80 ~

Is It Too Late?

Margaret Tyler felt nervous about her dinner date. After all, this was no ordinary man—this was her son, Jason. He was turning twenty-five tomorrow, and she had some apologies to make.

I wonder if he thinks I did everything wrong? she thought. Jason had been a challenging child. He had shown his strong and independent mind from infancy, and as he grew older he became more and more difficult to control. Margaret and her husband, Jim, were puzzled. Jason's siblings were well-behaved, showing what they considered normal levels of activity and "spunk." But Jason appeared in the family with a vengeance. He was like a human tornado. He was in constant motion, getting his hands on everything.

When Jason turned two, his temper tantrums demonstrated his single-minded goal of always getting his way. The fierceness of his determination was daunting to his sisters and brother, and even though he was the youngest, he became the family bully. He showed an amazing intelligence level, which made him even more difficult to control. He always seemed to be a couple steps ahead of his parents when it came to discipline and accountability. He was very good at figuring out the *letter* of the law. "You said not to jump off that chair," he would remind his mother. "I jumped off *this* chair."

During the first five years of his life, Jason's bent for nonstop action and adventure wore his mother down to the bone. Jim frequently stepped in and disciplined his son severely, but neither he nor Margaret had found a successful method for getting Jason to cooperate without a great deal of arguing, yelling, and punishment. Jim would often shake his head. "He *always* has a different idea," he marveled.

Once Jason started school, his incredible energy and activity level caused problems in the classroom almost immediately. Margaret shook her head in amazement, remembering those turbulent school years. *How did we even survive?* she wondered. A whole parade of teachers told them how much trouble Jason caused, how far behind he was getting in his work, and how casual his attitude was toward schoolwork.

Jason hated school. Looking back, Margaret wished she had tried harder to get to know Jason's teachers, to figure out why he was so unhappy in almost every class. *I know now,* she thought, *for all the good it does me.* She and Jim had spent much time arguing with Jason. They had threatened him, bribed him, and pleaded with him. They wanted him to get better grades, to keep his room clean, to run around with the right crowd. *We were sure we were right to be so hard on him,* Margaret mused. After all, parents were supposed to be in charge.

Despite their best efforts to control their son, in his sophomore year of high school Jason dropped out altogether. Margaret and Jim were devastated. None of their friends had ever had children who were high school dropouts! Jason then proceeded to rebel against virtually everything his parents valued. He was in and out of juvenile detention, and Margaret knew he was experimenting with drugs. He was always surrounded by friends who obviously looked to him for direction and leadership. "My friends respect and admire me," he had told her once. "That's more than my own family has ever done."

"Maybe that's because you've never shown respect for your *family*," she had snapped back. Margaret winced at the memory. Jason had been right—his family *didn't* respect him. In fact, they had spent his entire life insisting that he do things their way, instead of even trying to understand why he saw the world from such a different perspective.

Margaret sighed. Well, it had certainly been providential that she and her husband had attended a seminar and read a book about different learning styles. It made so much sense now! Jason had been pre-wired from the beginning to take in and process information from an entirely different perspective than either of his parents. His random, intuitive mind resisted checking off the list of chores posted on the refrigerator, or following the same bedtime routine, or obeying rules just because someone said so.

What a difference it would have made if only I had known about his learning style then! she thought. Both she and Jim agreed that they should at least *try* to talk to Jason about their new insights. It had been almost five years since Jason had communicated with them at all. He hadn't returned their phone messages, and all their notes and letters had gone unanswered. Margaret had left a different kind of message last week: "Jason, this is Mom. I'd like to invite you to dinner next Tuesday. Now wait—before you hang up on me, let me tell you that your father and I just want the opportunity to apologize to you for some things. We've just discovered what we did wrong, and we'd like to see if you agree. Will you call me?"

As she suspected, Jason found the invitation irresistible. Although he was reluctant, he agreed to come—but just for an hour or so. Now, at the sound of the doorbell, Margaret jumped to her feet. *This is it,* she told herself. *Please, God, don't let me blow it.*

"Hi, Mom." He looked thin, and Margaret struggled not to throw her arms around him.

"Jason, it's so good to see you!"

Jim walked into the living room and greeted his son carefully. As they all sat down, Jason looked at his parents. "So, what's the deal?"

Jim reached out and took his wife's hand. "Son, we need to apologize to you—not for the outcomes and accountability we held you to as a child, but for demanding that you meet those goals *our* way. We were wrong."

Jason looked surprised. Margaret spoke up.

"Jason, you were always an intelligent, gifted child. You didn't want to follow the rules, and we should have been more interested in the reasons why. If you'll give us a little time this evening, we'll tell you why we think you're going to be a very successful adult as you learn to use the gifts you've always had."

Jason shrugged. "Yeah, sure—whatever." But his eyes betrayed his interest.

This might just bring us back together, given enough time, thought Margaret. *Maybe it's not too late.* She smiled. *I have a feeling that when Jason gets married and has his own family, he's going to get a kid a lot like himself. He's going to need some advice!*

"Mom, could I have some coffee?"

Margaret quickly got to her feet. It was a start.

Recognize the Strength

Jason is like many troubled adolescents who feel misunderstood and under-appreciated for their talents. Many children simply don't fit into traditional classroom settings. But the very things that make them stand out uncomfortably during their school years can become their greatest assets later if those traits are carefully cultivated. Jason's natural leadership abilities and sense of adventure can become positive attributes for this young adult. It's never too late to help an adult who was unsuccessful as a child!

Focus on Accountability

If you find yourself needing to apologize to a wayward teenager who probably didn't deserve the harsh treatment he received when he or she was younger, be careful how you word your apology. You don't need to feel guilty or apologize for expecting high standards of behavior or moral outcomes for a child. What we as parents may find is that we were the most inflexible when we demanded our children accomplish *our goals* in *our way* only. If we can help them understand and commit to the end goal, we can then motivate them by using their own strengths and design.

It's Your Turn to Practice!

It's easy to forget, in the heat of the moment, how truly wonderful each of our children can be. Despite the frustration and inconvenience, they really are terrific kids! To help you focus on the strengths of each of your children, we've designed this quick form for you to fill out anytime you encounter a problem. Although it won't solve everything, it can start you out on the right foot and help maintain a positive relationship with your child while you work out the details! So photocopy a few to have on hand.

Date _____

Child's Name _____

1. Quick Reminder: What do I like best about this child? (Don't skip this one!)

2. What's the problem?

3. Which of my child's strengths are showing up in a negative way?

4. How can I direct those strengths so that they are being used productively?

5. How will I know that what I did works? (What's the point?)

∾ Bibliography ∾

Armstrong, Thomas. *The Myth of the A.D.D. Child: 50 Ways to Improve Your Child's Behavior and Attention Span Without Drugs, Labels, or Coercion.* New York: Dutton, 1995.

___. *7 Kinds of Smart.* New York: Penguin, 1993.

Barbe, Walter B. *Growing Up Learning.* Washington, D.C.: Acropolis, 1985.

Breggin, Peter and Ginger Ross Breggin. *The War Against Children: How the Drugs, Programs and Theories of the Psychiatric Establishment Are Threatening America's Children with a Medical "Cure" for Violence.* New York: St. Martin's, 1994.

Butler, Kathleen. *It's All in Your Mind: A Student's Guide to Learning Style.* Columbia, CT: The Learner's Dimension, 1988.

___. *Learning and Teaching Style: In Theory and Practice,* Second edition. Columbia, Conn.: The Learner's Dimension, 1988.

Chess, Stella, and Alexander Thomas. *Know Your Child.* New York: Basic, 1987.

Dunn, Rita and Kenneth Dunn. *Teaching Secondary Students Through Their Individual Learning Styles: Practical Approaches for Grades 7-12.* Boston: Allyn & Bacon, 1993.

Dunn, Rita, Kenneth Dunn, and Janet Perrin. *Teaching Young Children Through Their Individual Learning Styles: Practical Approaches for Grades K-2.* NY: St. John's University, 1993.

Gardner, Howard. *Frames of Mind: The Theory of Multiple Intelligences.* New York: Basic, 1983.

___. *The Unschooled Mind: How Children Think and How Schools Should Teach.* New York: Basic, 1991.

Gregorc, Anthony. *An Adult's Guide to Style,* Columbia, Conn.: Gregorc Associates, 1982.

Guild, Patricia and Stephen Garger. *Marching to Different Drummers.* Alexandria, VA: Association for Supervision and Curriculum Development, 1985.

Keirsey, David and Marilyn Bates. *Please Understand Me: Character and Temperment Types.* Del Mar, CA: Prometheus, Nemesis, 1978.

Kroeger, Otto and Janet M. Thuesen. *Type Talk.* New York: Delacorte Press, 1988.

Lawrence, Gordon. *People Types and Tiger Stripes: A Practical Guide to Learning Styles.* Gainesville, Fla.: Center for Applications of Psychological Type, Inc., 1993.

Lee, Christopher, and Rosemary Jackson. *Faking It: A Look into the Mind of a Creative Learner.* Portsmouth, N.H.: Boynton Cook, 1992.

Meisgeier, Charles and Elizabeth Murphy. *Murphy-Meisgeier Type Indicator for Children.* Palo Alto, Calif.: Consulting Psychologists Press, 1988.

Myers, Isabel Briggs. *Introduction to Type* (Rev. Ed.). Palo Alto, CA: Consulting Psychologists Press, Inc., 1987.

Owen, David. *None of the Above: Beyond the Myth of Scholastic Aptitude.* Boston: Houghton Mifflin, 1985.

Rusch, Shari Lyn. *Stumbling Blocks to Stepping Stones*. Seattle: Arc Press, 1991.

Simon, Anita and Claudia Byram. *You've Got to Reach 'em to Teach 'em*. Dallas: Training Associates, 1977.

Swindoll, Charles R. *You and Your Child: A Biblical Guide for Nurturing Confident Children From Infancy to Independence*. Nashville: Thomas Nelson, 1990.

Tobias, Cynthia Ulrich. *Every Child Can Succeed: Making the Most of Your Child's Learning Style*. Colorado Springs: Focus on the Family Publishing, 1996.

___. *The Way They Learn: How to Discover and Teach to Your Child's Strengths*. Colorado Springs: Focus on the Family Publishing, 1994.

___. *The Way We Work: A Practical Approach for Dealing with People on the Job*. Colorado Springs: Focus on the Family Publishing, 1995.

Tobias, Cynthia Ulrich with Nick Walker. *"Who's Gonna Make Me?" Effective Strategies for Dealing With the Strong-Willed Child*. (45-minute video) Seattle: Chuck Snyder & Associates, 1992.

Witkin, Herman and Donald R. Goodenough. *Cognitive Styles: Essence & Origins*. New York: International Universities Press, 1981.

Witkin, Herman, C.A. Moore, Donald R. Gooodenough, and P. W. Cox. "Field-Dependent and Field Independent Cognitive Styles and Their Educational Implications." Review of Educational Research 47 (Winter 1977): 1-64.

~ Favorite Children's Books ~

Brown, M.K. *Sally's Room*. New York: Scholastic: 1992.

Hazen, Barbara Shook. *Even If I Did Something Awful*. New York: Aladdin, 1992.

Henkes, Kevin. *Chester's Way*. New York: Puffin Books, 1988.

Lester, Helen. *Tacky the Penguin*. Boston: Houghton Mifflin, 1988.

Scieszka, Jon and Lane Smith. *Math Curse*. New York: Viking, 1995.